I0753117

DODGE'S PASS & TROOPER'S MOUNT, W. T.
The outer Rampart.

THE
BLACK HILLS.

A MINUTE DESCRIPTION OF THE

ROUTES, SCENERY, SOIL, CLIMATE, TIMBER,
GOLD, GEOLOGY, ZOÖLOGY, ETC.

WITH

AN ACCURATE MAP, FOUR SECTIONAL DRAWINGS,
AND TEN PLATES FROM PHOTOGRAPHS,
TAKEN ON THE SPOT.

BY
RICHARD IRVING DODGE,
LIEUT.-COLONEL, U. S. ARMY.

NEW YORK:
JAMES MILLER, PUBLISHER,
647 BROADWAY.
1876.

New York: Lange, Little & Co., Printers.
Nos. 10 to 20 Astor Place.

PREFACE.

SINCE my return from the exploration of the Black Hills last October, I have been so repeatedly and earnestly importuned by persons desirous of information in regard to that country, that I have felt, as it were, forced to give an account of what was discovered therein.

This little volume is given to the public in deference to the general anxiety for a reliable and authentic statement.

It has been thrown together in the intervals of public and private duties of much graver importance; but, while asserting no claim to literary merit, it may be relied on as in strict and impartial accordance with facts.

THE AUTHOR.

CONTENTS.

ILLUSTRATIONS.

The Black Hills.

IT is scarcely seventy years since a little party, numbering less than twenty individuals, and led by two Captains of the United States Army, started from the then almost extreme frontier town of St. Louis, to find a route to the Pacific Ocean.

Painfully "tracking" the heavily loaded boats against the swift current of the grandest branch of the "Father of Waters," slowly and patiently this party plodded on, making in a month scarce greater distance than the lordly steamboat now makes in a day.

Where now stand goodly towns and cities, was then an unknown wilderness, uninhabited, except by savage beasts, or scarcely less savage tribes of Indians.

The way opened, and the fur-trade with the Indians proving most lucrative, hundreds of adventurers poured into the country. These men traveled on horseback or on foot, carrying their necessaries and accumulated peltries packed on the backs of animals. They generally wandered along the streams, as led by fancy, or the probable abundance of fur animals. They cared nothing for roads or maps, and, being themselves ignorant, added but little to the general stock of knowledge of this immense "terra incognita."

It was not until the discovery of gold in California, and subsequently in Colorado and elsewhere in these great western wastes, that regular lines of travel were adopted.

From the nature of the country and the paucity of feasible passes through the great Rocky Mountain ranges, these roads were very few, and were, moreover, confined to a comparatively narrow north and south belt.

It is not to be wondered at therefore, if, even at this late day, and in this age of exploration, there are yet vast portions of our own wide territory as absolutely unknown to the scientific and map-making world, as any part of the densely-peopled wilderness of Africa.

Far out of the ordinary lines of plains travel, surrounded on all sides by the arid wastes of the "Bad Lands," by bands of hostile and treacherous savages, the "Black Hills" loomed up in silent majesty, mysterious, unknown.

Though many had, afar off, gazed in wistful wonder at the long black mass, no white man had ever penetrated their recesses, or bared the secrets hidden in their dark bosoms.

The Indians, the supposed dwellers in this land, maintained, when questioned about it, the most studied silence, or, even in their most confidential or drunken moments, gave such evasive and unsatisfactory replies as added tenfold to the strength of the mysterious fascination which existed in regard to it.

For more than twenty years the name "Black Hills" has been to the plains traveler the embodiment of the fullest idea of the mysterious and the unknown.

The disposition to penetrate the unknown is, to some natures, the strongest of passions. Yet every effort to open up this country became abortive, in the face of the thousand difficulties and dangers which beset the would-be explorer.

At last came in that strongest of all human incentives, the love of gold. Some Indians came into a frontier trading-post, bringing small grains and nuggets of the shining metal.

Plied with presents and whisky, they said it came from the "Black Hills." The story spread, gaining in force and volume, exciting all classes of people, until the Government determined on the solution of the question.

Custer's expedition of 1874 was the result. The very short time allowed for the exploration was, probably, the cause of an unfortunate disagreement in the reports of the military and scientific heads of the expedition.

The question, gold or not, still remained unsettled, and the country almost feverishly agitated on the subject.

Another expedition was ordered for 1875. A scientific party, headed by Mr. Jenney, was sent out by the Interior Department, with means and time to make a thorough survey. An ample force of troops was sent for the protection of this party.

No one but a lover of the plains and of plains life, and who has himself some of that passion for "penetrating the unknown," can realize all the pleasure with which the writer received his billet to be one of the expedition.

On most maps of "the plains" the name "Black Hills" is given to two entirely different and widely separate portions of country.

The "Black Hills" proper are not visible from any place or point on the old overland stage-road to Salt Lake and California, but the name was already in the mouths of travelers, as the wildest and most mysterious of the unknown regions to be traversed. As the stage bowled along, day after day, on that long and tedious route, the Jehus were constantly asked, "Where are the Black Hills?" and in default of the real article they pointed out the long range of mountains on the east and north of the Laramie Plains; and by many persons in that section, and on most maps, the splendid "Laramie Range," the most easterly of the Rocky Mountains, and in crossing which the locomotive reaches its greatest altitude in North America, and, with one or two exceptions, in the world, is now called by the very insignificant title "the Black Hills."

More than two hundred miles east of north of the "Laramie Range," in the midst of a desert of dreary alkaline plains, rises a magnificent mass of mountains, covering a country almost as large as the State of Vermont, and closely embraced within the two principal branches of the Cheyenne river.

To this country all the tribes of the great Dakota or Sioux Nation give the name "Pah-sappa," which, literally interpreted, is "black hill;" Pah—hill, sappa—black.

The expedition was organized at Fort Laramie, from which post we expected to re-supply ourselves from time to time with such stores as might be necessary.

Fort Laramie is the oldest of the present frontier military posts.

Many years ago it was a station of the Hudson Bay

Company. On the nominal expulsion of that company from United States territory, it became a station and trading-post of the American Fur Company.

In 1849 it was first occupied by the United States as a military post, and being in a commanding position with reference to the surrounding Indian tribes, it has been, and still is, of very considerable importance.

The post is prettily situated on the left bank of the Laramie river, about two miles from its junction with the North Platte, and just at the foot of the northeastern slope of the great Laramie Range of the Rocky Mountains (sometimes, as heretofore stated, erroneously called the Black Hills).

The country in the vicinity is very broken, barren, and entirely unfit for agricultural purposes.

It is, however, fairly covered with grass, and is pretty well adapted to stock raising.

Both the Platte and Laramie are fine rivers, the former large and deep, and flowing with a tremendous current. A fine bridge (since completed) was in course of construction by the Government, but we were obliged to trust ourselves to a very shaky ferry-boat, which, however, I ought not to abuse, as it carried us all over safely.

We left Fort Laramie on the 25th of May, traveling north across the long rolling slopes of the high plains, skirting the base of a huge isolated granite mass called Rawhide Peak, which rises six thousand five hundred feet above tide-water, and on the third day reached the head springs of the Niobrara, or "Running Water."

The country in the vicinity of this stream, though monotonous, is yet very beautiful at this season. The slopes are long and gentle, covered with grass green as emerald, and dotted with flowers in great variety, while the air is vocal with the songs of birds. Hundreds of bobolinks tumble in short eccentric flights through the air, each pouring forth his ecstatic song, while field-larks and blackbirds swell the chorus of voices, giving life and love and song even to the wilderness. Nowhere in our whole expedition did we find such an abundance of singing birds as welcomed us to the valley of the Niobrara.

Still continuing north over fine rolling grass-covered prairie, most attractive in appearance, and gradually ascending, we came in about nine miles to an abrupt descent, at the bottom of which, a thousand feet below us, is the branch of the Cheyenne river called the "Old Woman's Fork."

This name, a literal translation of the Indian name of this stream, is said to be derived from a tradition of the Sioux, that an old insane woman wandered from the camp and was never seen or heard of again in life. They believe that she died; that her spirit haunts the high hills and knolls which border the stream. She is always in white, like a civilized ghost, and may frequently be seen on clear starlight nights dancing alone on a high, flat-topped hill, a detached portion of the great plain; or her voice may be heard chanting the monotonous songs of the Indian. She does no harm, and it is rather "good medicine" to see or hear her.

The scenery from the top of the divide above "Old Woman's Fork" is most beautiful and striking in its variety. To the south and southeast stretch the apparently level green plains. In front, and to the right and left, is the profound abyss, its edges broken into a thousand forms by the action of the elements, and dotted with pines singly or in groups, in picturesque irregularity. Further north the ground falls away in long slopes, cut by myriads of ravines, to the Cheyenne, and bounding the horizon in that direction is the long line of "Black Hills," the unknown haven of our hopes.

The usual description of travel, "we went north," or "we followed the creek," has little significance to those persons who are accustomed to travel by good roads as many miles in a day as would, with great exertion and good fortune, be made in two, three, four, or even five days of plains travel. No one but a plains traveler, one accustomed to make roads for himself, can realize the care, judgment, skill, and hard labor expressed in these phrases.

Persons not familiar with the plains, assuming the name as indicative of their actual surface, imagine it an easy matter to move from one to another portion of the country. There is no greater error. The plains are such, generally, only in name. The lack of trees exposes them peculiarly to the action of the elements, and nowhere can one find more irregularity of surface, more abrupt ascents and precipitous descents, more broken, jagged, and apparently impassable country than on the plains. Nowhere do the rains cut more deeply, nowhere do frosts split more perpendicular faces. The beds of most of the streams are quagmires, or the more tenacious and dangerous quicksand. Banks are to be cut down, narrow, sharp ridges to be leveled off, bridges and corduroys to be constructed; every mile gained is a record of plains craft and intelligent labor. Our journey down the "Old Woman's Fork" demanded the display of the utmost of these qualities.

The high mésa on the south and east of the "Old Woman's Fork" was undoubtedly once the bank or shore of a great lake of the tertiary period. The creek itself runs through what was then the bed of the lake. The slopes and hills on each side are filled with fossils in wonderful variety and abundance. The water is good, but there is no arable land. This valley can never be valuable for agriculture, but the "bottom" furnishes numerous lovely sites for stock ranches, and the whole country is covered with magnificent grass.

Traveling east of north we in two days reached the Cheyenne river, here a nasty stream of thick milky water, scarcely fit for the use of man, but eagerly drunk by our animals. The valley of the south Cheyenne is from half a mile to a mile in width. It is well covered with young cotton-wood, the older trees having been cut down by Indians for horse-feed in winter. Valley and hills are covered with abundant and good grass, and the country will support immense herds of cattle. The hills on each side are tertiary deposits, containing many fossils. In some places there is the usual "bad land" formation. There are also great beds of gypsum, but none especially pure or valuable.

The stream is exceedingly crooked, winding in intricate curves from hill to hill, and changing its character at almost every bend. In some places it is narrow, with mud banks and bottom, in others it is a sandy bed, sometimes three or four hundred feet wide, and filled with quicksands.

Traveling down the Cheyenne for two days, and then north one day, through tertiary deposits, we gained Beaver Creek, which we followed up one day, and then struck for the mountains.

The Beaver is a clear, pretty-looking stream of horrible alkaline water, full of all abominable tastes, and unfit for drinking or cooking. Its volume, where first we struck it, is about one thousand miners' inches. All the country south is "bad land" or tertiary formation, much cut by deep and abrupt ravines. From its north bank stretches a barren plain, bounded at a distance of from two to five miles by a line of steep and rugged hills from four to eight hundred feet above the plain—the "outer rampart" of the Black Hills.

Over the tops of these appear ridge after ridge, mountain upon mountain, until the grand black mass blends with the blue of the skies.

The Beaver is fringed with a scanty growth of cotton-wood, some of which are quite large, and in their branches are occasional Indian graves.

There is nothing in which the plains Indian varies so greatly as in the respect paid to the dead. This variation is not in the customs of different bands or tribes, all being very much alike, but seems to be due entirely to circumstances.

During the long enforced inaction of the winter camp, which the "Noble Red Man" must get through as best he can in gambling and sleep, the death of some prominent person is almost a matter of rejoicing. All may indulge the luxury of grief, and from the commencement of the elaborate preparations to the final ceremony, the funeral excitement may last for quite a month.

The death of the same person in the summer would cause some little excitement, and possibly a day or two might be given to the obsequies; but should he be so unfortunate as to die during the fall hunt, or while on some important expedition, the body would likely be thrust without ceremony into the first convenient hole in the rocks or prairie.

The favorite burying-place of all the plains Indians is a tree.

A platform is made in the branches and the body disposed upon it, sometimes in a sitting posture, but generally lying on the back.

It is dressed in such articles of civilized clothing as deceased possessed in life, or as are bestowed by the kindness and piety of friends. His arms, blankets, some cooking-utensils, food, matches, etc., whatever may be necessary on the long journey, or to enable him to make a presentable appearance in the "Happy Hunting Grounds," are placed on the platform with the body. Light branches are bent from side to side like the bows of a wagon, and the whole closely covered with rawhide.

In the absence of trees of sufficient size, four light poles are set in the ground, and the platform constructed on their tops, sometimes only six or eight feet from the ground, scarcely beyond the reach of the hungry wolves which soon collect about it.

The Sioux on the Reservations now frequently use

INDIAN GRAVES. BELLE FOURCHE.

the boxes in which stores are sent to them, or obtaining a few pieces of board, put together a rude coffin, which, with the body, is mounted on poles, as described.

There is no special burying-place, even near a camp as permanent as Indians ever make. Each head of a family buries his dead wherever he pleases, so it be at some distance. The vicinity of such a camp is frequently dotted with graves, generally each by itself.

The cut represents the only group of such graves I have ever seen, though it is by no means unusual to find ten or fifteen graves in a specially favorable tree.

The Sioux seem to attach some special importance to green as a funereal color. In almost all the graves examined by our party, the blankets in which the remains were wrapped were green.

On one of the constant pack-mule surveys made by small parties detached from the main body of the expedition, one of the scientific gentlemen found that his horse's back had become sore, and that another saddle-blanket was absolutely necessary to keep the animal in a serviceable condition. An Indian grave was examined, and the dry bones found wrapped in a good green blanket.

After some natural hesitation the blanket was appropriated as the Indian contribution to science.

The horse's back improved, and all went swimmingly until the party began to encounter small bodies of Indians, all very friendly, and demonstrative in hand-shakings. Each man of such parties scrutinized, narrowly and anxiously, first the green blanket, then the person of the individual riding on the saddle, which covered but did not conceal it. This occurred so frequently and was so noticeable that our scientific friend became extremely nervous, and the "conscience which makes cowards of us all" so worked upon him, that when he saw at a distance an approaching party of Indians, he immediately found something specially important in another direction. The others of the party made great sport of the poor fellow's predicament, and gave him the Indian name "Wa-shenar-kokape," which being interpreted, means, "The-man-afraid-of-his-blankets."

Of course he could have avoided all this by simply throwing away the blanket; but then his horse was likely to become unserviceable, and being an extremely zealous and conscientious man, he preferred the personal risk to the chance of official or scientific failure.

As we go up the Beaver the country gets in every way worse. A dreary, monotonous, alkaline plain, no timber except an occasional scrubby cotton-wood. The water, acrid and bitter, irritating to the mouth, throat, and alimentary canal, stands in long, narrow, and deep pools, in which there seems to be no life, either animal or vegetable. Every man was more or less affected, and all were glad to turn our faces to what seems a gap in the apparently impenetrable mass of mountains to the north.

A few hours brought us to this gorge, when we went into camp in a spot which, after our trying journey over the horrible alkaline desert, seemed a paradise.

A lovely stream, of apparently pure water, rushed swiftly from its mountain home, through a grassy mead, smooth as a lawn, green as emerald, and carpeted with flowers of every hue. Overhanging the stream, and dotted singly or in clumps about the lawn were hundreds of box-elder, the most graceful and picturesque of plains trees. Just at the entrance of a narrow cañon, the mountains to east and west tower to the height of from one thousand to fifteen hundred feet, their summits and the deep gorges scored in their sides clothed with dark forests of pine.

The brook was named Spaulding's Creek. The spot, Camp Jenney. It is one of the most beautiful camps I ever saw. There we remained for some days, and here we acquired our earliest ideas of the Black Hills.

Reconnaisances on horseback were made in every direction, to discover, if possible, a practicable route for our wagons.

Whatever may be inside, nature seems to have taken the utmost pains to protect it from the knowledge of man. The immense wall of mountains to the eastward offered not the slightest vantage-ground to the intruder. After long and diligent search a game trail was discovered leading in the right direction. Following it with difficulty, we climbed range after range, rising one above the other, and separated by ravines and cañons, more or less deep and precipitous, until no less than six apparent ranges had been surmounted, and we had reached an altitude of about two thousand feet above the valley, or nearly seven thousand feet above tide-water. Here we found ourselves on a comparative level, covered with pine forest more or less dense. In front, the ground descended gently, and nearly a mile ahead, on the same level, was a low ridge which shut out the view. Going down a long, gentle slope, and up a long, gentle slope, we reached this ridge, only to find another exactly similar in advance.

After thus passing four ridges, and seeing nothing but ridges still in advance, we turned back, having fully demonstrated the impracticability of any wagon-route in this direction, for, even were it possible to drag the wagons over the almost precipitous ranges, there was no water.

This western rim of the Black Hills is an immense mésa of secondary formation, the top being carboniferous limestone. The lines of easiest abrasion are north and south, or parallel to Spaulding's Creek, and the five or six apparent ranges, each to the east overtopping that to the west, are only portions of the same original mésa, detached by the subsequent action of the elements. The water falling on the surface has cut depressions, deepening into gorges, which wind and twist most irregularly, but maintain a general parallelism to the original face of the upheaval. At last, many of them uniting, they have been able to force their way directly through the opposing ridges, and gain for their waters an outlet to Spaulding's Creek.

The cañons thus cut are magnificent in their abrupt profundity, many being not less than twelve to fifteen hundred feet in depth, while scarce half that width at the top. The openings of the cañons into the main valley are extremely disproportioned in width to their depth, length, and the volume of water which must sometimes be poured from them. In front of these narrow doors, the valley of the main creek is covered with débris, drift-wood, and boulders of all sizes. In some cases the force of the water has been so great as to carry huge rocks, five or six feet in diameter, for quite a mile out on the plain, while the sand and mud deposited by the abating currents have built transverse beds many feet higher than the general level of the valley.

It is practically impossible to enter the "Hills" to the east or northeast of Camp Jenney with wagons.

A few days' sojourn at Camp Jenney proved to us that the water, clear, cold, and pure to the taste, was yet full of alkaline impurities, which affected almost every one injuriously. Besides this, the geology of this section proving very simple, the scientific party were soon ready for further exploration.

Camp Jenney is in the Red Valley. For about twelve miles above, this valley and the valley of Spaulding's Creek are the same.

No route practicable for wagons having been discovered by any of the exploring parties, it was decided that our best chance for a good route is to follow up this creek, rising with it, and thus gradually reach the summit of the immense table of rock, which here presents an insurmountable barrier to our progress towards the heart of the Hills.

The valley scarce averages half a mile in width, and is bounded on each side by almost precipices, of from one to two thousand feet. The eastern mountain sends into the main creek numbers of clear, beautiful brooklets, which, though cool as ice and very palatable, are poison to the stomach, containing gypsum, salt, and a thousand impurities, borrowed from the red and gypsum beds. These brooks, in making their way across the valley to the main stream, have, as it were, dammed themselves up by a constant deposit of their own impurities; throwing the water out of its beds and overflowing the valley.

These deposits, a yellowish, soft, porous travertine, vary in thickness, sometimes reaching several feet. When dry they are sufficiently strong to bear a horse, but when wet, they give way beneath his step or the wheel of a wagon. Our train soon made difficult bogs of these places.

The scenery is very grand and beautiful. The valley, owing to the number of streams, is a rich green. On each side rise ranges from one to two thousand feet, their tops covered with the dark, thick growth of pine which gives the name "Black" to the "Hills." The face of these ranges shows near their tops a stratum of several hundred feet of red sandstone; below this, a belt of very uniform thickness of white limestone; below this, a greenish formation, which the geologists pronounce "Jurassic;" near the bottom are beds of great thickness, of a stiff red clay; and against the base of these are immense dirty-white beds of gypsum; below all is the green valley, graceful with trees and shrubbery. The combination and variety of colors, the towering precipices and broken crags, make a picture as delightful to the eye as may be found.

In our progress up Spaulding's Creek, we rose at the rate of nearly a hundred feet to the mile. At about twelve miles from Camp Jenney the valley of Spaulding's Creek becomes a cañon, very narrow and deep, while the Red Valley, rising over a series of long rounded slopes, trends to the westward and widens out to several miles.

The topographical features are here very remarkable, mountain and plain, forest and prairie, smooth level surfaces and rocky deep cañons being all jumbled together. We stand on a high, level, treeless plain, apparently limitless to the west and northwest; behind us are the long slopes terminating in the valley from which we have recently emerged; in front, and on the same level with us is a heavy mass of pine forest; to the east, immediately on our right, is the cañon of Spaulding's Creek, five hundred feet deep, and impassable for anything but a bird; and close from its further brink, broken and precipitous mountains, covered with dense black forests of pine, rise yet a thousand feet above us.

Our route led along the brink of the cañon of Spaulding's Creek, from the almost precipitous sides of which gushed numerous springs of pure water. One of these, which could be got at by animals, was evidently a favorite resort of Indians, as many camps were found, of all ages. This we named "Indian Spring."

Still keeping close to the cañon we were, in a few miles further, gratified by seeing other ravines and cañons breaking away from us to tne west, assuring us that we were on a true "divide" or water shed. This divide now began to turn toward the east, and we were soon crawling up a narrow backbone, the cañons of Spaulding's Creek on our right, those of some yet unknown stream on our left.

After a mile of not very difficult climbing we reached the summit, seven thousand four hundred feet above tide-water, and were rewarded with an indescribably magnificent view, the whole country being spread out like a map at our feet. The Black Hills were open to us, but as the Promised Land was open to Moses, to sight only. Stretching away to the right and left, and on the same general level as the ground on which we stood, was the great mesa, the surmounting of which had presented so many obstacles. In front, and apparently far below us, was a confused mass of mountain and gorge, without system or order, and presenting not the slightest appearance of opening or valley, through or by which we might hope to make a way for our wagons.

However, "needs must." We plunged down the deep and precipitous descent, and, after some miles of intricate and difficult travel emerged on a narrow valley through which ran a wagon road—"Custer's trail." Here we found splendid springs of most delicious water, and encamped.

An examination of Custer's map shows us that we

are now in what he named "Floral Valley," described by him as more profusely bedecked with flowers than any other portion of the Hills seen by him. He passed in July. We camp here on the 11th of June. It is a pretty little gorge even now, a level "bottom" of eighty to one hundred yards, bounded on each side by abrupt hills, five to eight hundred feet in height, and densely covered with pine, spruce, and quaking asp. But, alas for the "floral" valley! Spring has as yet scarce touched the earth, which is saturated with moisture from the melting snow; not a flower is to be seen; the buds on those trees and bushes which have southern exposure are just swelling; the "bottom" is of a pale, sickly green, from the scarcely started grass.

Hardly had our tents been pitched, when a furious storm of mingled rain and snow drove all but the guards to shelter. The unfortunate animals were soon covered with a blanket of sleet, and, having no food, presented by morning a most miserable and dejected aspect. We have all good cause to remember "Floral Valley."

It is not my purpose to attempt to follow the expedition in all its windings, its explorations, its labors, its troubles, and its pleasures; but so to sum up the information gained as to give an idea, as perfect as possible, of the nature of the country, its climate, soil, resources, and value.

GEOLOGY.

The following most interesting remarks on the geological structure of the Black Hills were kindly furnished me by Mr. Henry Newton, the accomplished assistant geologist of the expedition, who devoted to the subject a whole summer of close study, and labor so patient and so indefatigable that it would be hardly too much to say that there is scarcely a rock in the whole length and breadth of the "Hills" which does not bear the mark of his hammer.

STRUCTURE OF THE BLACK HILLS.

The rocks forming the Black Hills consist of three classes; the older metamorphic sediments—now slates and schists; the more recent unchanged sedimentary strata, the sandstones, limestones, clays, etc., resting upon the former unconformably; and the rocks of igneous origin, the granites, feldspar, porphyries, etc. These strata are exposed in the Hills in the following order descending:

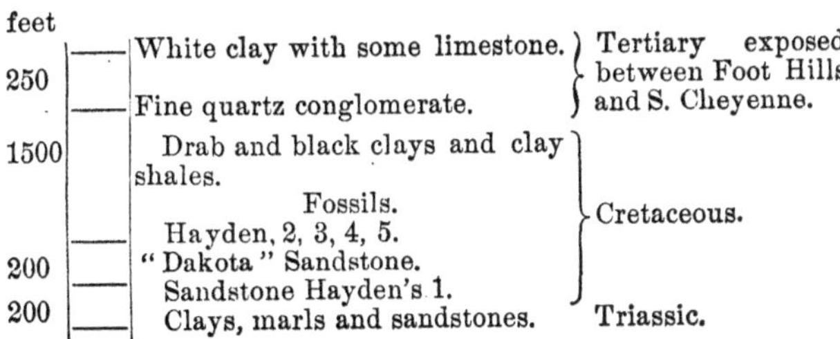

feet		
	White clay with some limestone.	Tertiary exposed between Foot Hills and S. Cheyenne.
250		
	Fine quartz conglomerate.	
1500	Drab and black clays and clay shales. Fossils. Hayden, 2, 3, 4, 5.	Cretaceous.
200	"Dakota" Sandstone. Sandstone Hayden's 1.	
200	Clays, marls and sandstones.	Triassic.

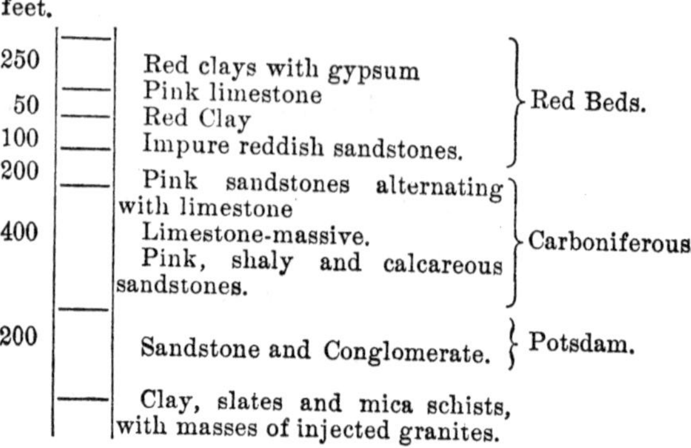

I. The oldest rocks, geologically, are the schists and slates which form the nucleal area of the Hills, a widely elliptical region, about twenty miles wide and forty miles long, north and south. These are mainly of sedimentary origin, but have been metamorphosed by cosmical forces into micaceous, garnetiferous, and argillaceous and silicious slates and schists. Of these the micaceous and garnetiferous schists of the Harney's Peak region appear to be of greater age than the argillaceous and silicious slates further north, as one or two localities seem to show their unconformability. These rocks contain very numerous seams of quartz, ferruginous quartz, and quartzite, which have been found in some cases to carry free gold, and it is probable that all the gold found in the gravels and sands of the streams running through these rocks was originally derived from this source.

This
Page
is
Blank

Materials were not available when scanned.

This Page is Blank

Materials were not available when scanned.

At various places in the area of the metamorphic schists and slates are masses of feldspathic granite, as Harney's Peak and vicinity, and beyond the same, of feldspathic porphyry, as Terry's Peak, Inyan Kara, Crow Peak, Bare Peak, Sun Dance Hills, Bear Lodge, Little Missouri Buttes, etc., which have been injected through the superincumbent strata at the time of the elevation of the range.

The approximate time of this injection I have previously thought to be between the close of the Cretaceous and the opening of the Tertiary age, though further proof is wanted to establish this fact. Further mention of these igneous centers will be made when speaking of the order of events in the building up of the Black Hills. In rudely concentric order around the area of slates, unconformably upon them, lie the later sedimentary rocks, beginning with

II.—The Potsdam Formation. Unconformably upon these metamorphic slates, etc., and surrounding the nucleal area, lies a mass of reddish or reddish-brown sandstone, often at the base conglomerate, in some places formed of large boulders from the area of slates, which from the fossil remains is referable to the Potsdam formation of the lower Silurian age. This formation is variable in thickness—from ten to two hundred and fifty feet—being thicker at the north, in the vicinity of Terry's and Warren's Peaks, and thinnest at the southern end of the Hills.

Sometimes the sandstones are found changed into a hard quartzite, where the igneous rocks at the time of their injection have penetrated into and abutted against them.

Fossil remains, algæ, mollusks, etc., have been found in this formation in the Hills, excelling in their abundance and beauty of preservation those from the most noted localities of the formation in the east.

III.—The Carboniferous Formation has a very great development in the Black Hills, forms a very important feature in their geology, and gives character to much of their topography. The mass of the formation is a limestone of a white or pinkish color, of different degrees of purity, silicious, especially near the top, and changing above into an alternation of pinkish sandstones and limestones, a transition to the sandstones of the Red Beds.

The thickness of the formation is greatest in the northern half of the hills, where it becomes four hundred to five hundred feet thick. Though the same geological horizon in the Mississippi Valley bears many valuable seams of coal, it is, over most of the area of the great West, as in the Black Hills, a limestone containing no coal, the product of deposition in a deep sea. Surrounding the Hills in a thick stratum, covering often large areas, and inclining rarely at an angle exceeding ten or fifteen degrees, the outgoing streams draining the interior area, have cut through it and the overlying Red Beds in long, deep, and rugged cañons, which are a most interesting and wild feature in the topography of the Hills, and which prevent on almost all sides easy entrance into and passage through them. From the base of the mésa, which forms the western border of the nucleal area of slates for a long distance, and which is mainly formed of the Carboniferous limestone, rise in springs most of the streams draining the Hills in a west and east direction. From the observations of Dr. V. T. McGillycuddy, topographer, the "Monument," an elevated point of carboniferous limestone on the mésa, near Floral Valley, is the highest point in the Black Hills, being seven thousand six hundred feet above the sea, or one hundred and forty feet above Harney's Peak.

Fossils are not abundant in the limestones of this formation, but a sufficient number of characteristic species were obtained to fix accurately its geological position.

IV.—Next in ascending order are the Red Beds, which are so interesting a feature in the geology of the whole Rocky Mountain range, from the Rio Grande on the south to the far north. Though fossil remains have been found in but very few localities in the whole area of their exposure in the west, and none whatever by our expedition, from their general lithological character and their relation to the underlying Carboniferous and overlying Jurassic, this formation has been generally known by American geologists as the Triassic. The unusual absence of fossil remains is probably explained by the fact that the sediments composing the formation are the result of a deposition in shallow and very brackish waters in which animal life was scarce or entirely absent. In these notes I have included in this group—the Red Beds—the following members, beginning below—a heavy mass, two hundred feet or more, of impure sandstones of a variegated pink and red color, which are separated by some seventy-five feet of red clay from a purple limestone about forty-five feet in thickness, above which lies a heavy mass, two hundred to two hundred and fifty feet in thickness, of red clay, containing immense beds of gypsum. Some geologists maintain that the purple limestone and overlying red clays and gypsum should be included with the Jurassic, but as yet we have no palæontological evidence for this division, and hence I have included them all under the name of *Red Beds.*

This pink or purple limestone is a peculiarly interesting member of the geological series, as it forms the outer slope of so large a portion of the timbered area of the hills. This is finely illustrated by the broad, rising slopes from Inyan Kara eastward toward Camp Transfer, and from the Red Water Valley southward into the northern end of the Hills. The red clays with gypsum which overlie this limestone, are probably the most interesting element in the entire geological series represented in the Hills. From their persistency and high color, with their numerous strata of snowy-white gypsum, encircling the Hills on all sides in a broad belt, they form a picturesque feature from whatever side the Hills are approached. The wonderful red valley, that encompasses the Hills as a moat or ditch surrounds a fortress, is wholly cut in these beds, which, being soft and easily eroded, have been cut out and washed away by the rains and the draining streams. This valley, widening out at the north and northwest, forms the valley of the Red Water and the great area between the Sun Dance Hills and Inyan Kara. Another area has also been discovered occupying the valley of the Belle Fourche for a long distance above and below the Devil's Tower.

V.—The Jurassic. The beds of clay, marl, and sandstone forming the base and in some places the greater part of the escarpment-like hills that overlook the Red Valley and surround the fortress of the Black Hills, were from their fossil remains recognized by Professors Meek and Hayden, in 1858, as of Jurassic age. These beds, though varying somewhat in character, are found to be continuously exposed in the foot-hills. In the northwest they thicken out very remarkably and occupy a large area between Sun Dance Hills, Warren's Peak and the Devil's Tower.

VI.—THE CRETACEOUS. The Cretaceous formation is formed at its base of a series of yellowish and reddish sandstones, the Dakota group, more or less massive, capping the cordon or escarpment of foot-hills that surrounds the Black Hills proper. Above this is a great thickness of black and drab clays and clay shales which slope off gradually on all sides, and underlie a large area of the plains in Dakota and Wyoming. This Cretaceous area surrounds the Hills in a broad belt, and by the valley of the Cheyenne is connected with the Cretaceous deposits of the Upper Missouri. Beyond this wide rim of Cretaceous, the plains are underlaid by beds of Tertiary age. Certain of these beds contain considerable quantities of crystallized gypsum or selenite, which may be seen for miles glistening in the sunlight, and large amounts of soluble salts, alkalies, which contaminate most of the streams running through them. At certain localities of the exposures of these beds on the Cheyenne and its branches quite a large number of beautifully-colored and preserved shells, common forms of the Cretaceous, were obtained.

VII.—THE TERTIARY. Of the Tertiary formation there exists but a very limited area immediately embraced in the region of our survey of the last summer, and this occupies a narrow strip between the

North & South Section-Black Hills.

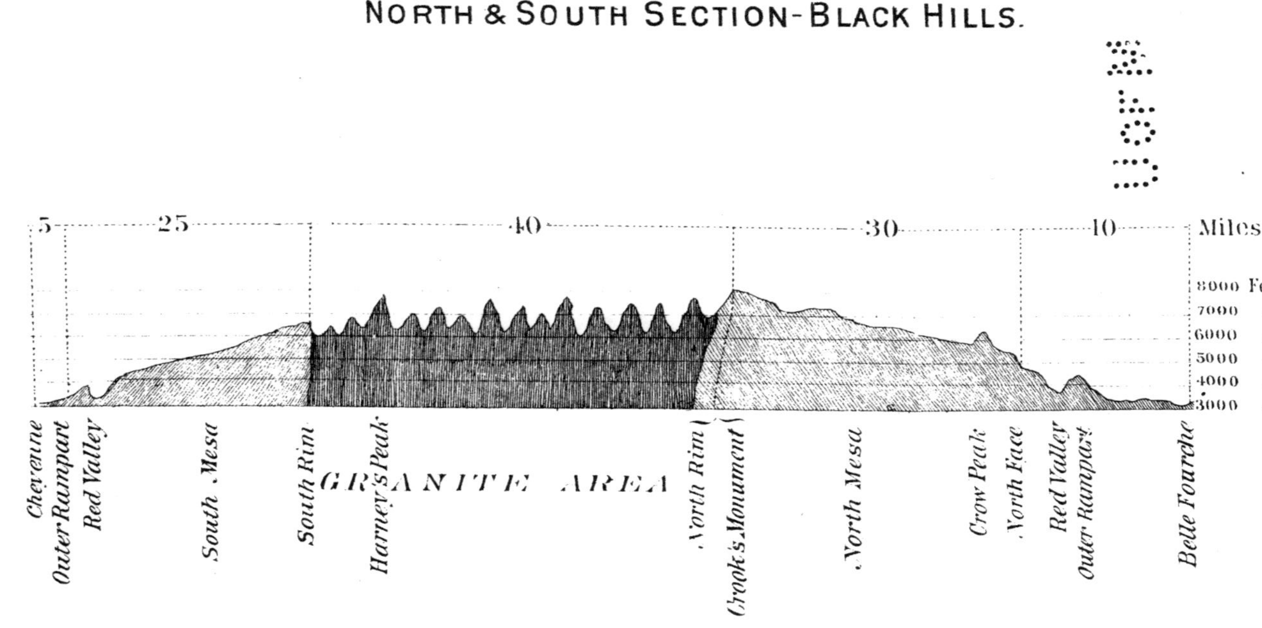

south Cheyenne and the foot-hills, from Rapid south to French Creek. Where examined it did not attain a thickness above two hundred or three hundred feet, composed at base of a stratum eight to ten feet of fine water-worn quartz gravel, on which rests a series of light-colored clays with some impure limestone. Everywhere large quantities of white chalcedony are found covering the surface, which formerly filled crevices and seams in the mass of the formation. This area appears to have been a fresh-water deposit, once probably connected with the Tertiary (Bad Lands) east of the Cheyenne river. On account of the very slight dip of both the Cretaceous and Tertiary toward the east, in this region, no unconformability of dip could be discovered between them, though it was earnestly looked for. Beyond the area of Cretaceous, already mentioned, encircling the Hills, the plains are underlaid for great distances by the Tertiary, westward toward the Big Horn and Powder river region, southward to and beyond the Pacific Railroad, and eastward occupying most of the distance to the Missouri river. This formation, which along the White and Niobrara rivers is remarkable for the fossil vertebrate remains, was found to be wholly barren when examined west of the Cheyenne. An area of vertebrate fossils in the Bad Lands was, however, passed through between the Cheyenne and the White rivers, which excels in richness any area of the "*Bone Fields*" heretofore known.

VIII.—Drift. Over large areas, especially on the north and east side of the Hills, these being most thoroughly examined, the surface to, and even beyond the Cheyenne, is scattered with small fragments and pebbles of the harder rocks of the Black Hills, sometimes several feet in thickness, and, in some instances, near the Cheyenne river, masses many hundred pounds in weight, of quartzite, etc., are found lying on the surface. Even so far eastward as between the Cheyenne and White rivers, pieces of the granite rock, rose quartz, etc., peculiar to the Black Hills, were found sparingly scattered on the surface. Though we could find in the Hills proper no indubitable evidence of glacial action, still, the presence of these fragments mentioned would seem to require some transporting force greater than that of water, and this I consider to have been *ice*. We have no reason to doubt that the glacial period enshrouded all this region with ice, but that it should have left so few marks of its presence is at present somewhat of a problem; though perhaps an immense ice sheet, with little motion, and dissolving away in a sea, produced by depression of the land, would explain some of the facts.

Of the operation of more recent geological forces in denuding, cutting out valleys, channels, and cañons, of which there are such fine exhibitions in the Black Hills, perhaps there need be nothing said, as they are simple and plain phenomena producing the present topographical features.

In order to give a more complete idea of the general geological structure of the Black Hills than can be conveyed by a mere description, a rude cross-section of the Hills from east to west, near Harney's Peak, is given below.

SEQUENCE OF EVENTS OF FORMATION.

In conclusion, I would add only a brief synopsis of what, at present, appears to me to have been the sequence of events in the formation and elevation of the Black Hills.

First. The elevation of the schists and metamorphic slates, produced by one or oft repeated forces of elevation, forming, finally, an island near where Harney's Peak now stands, and a low ridge or reef, south and north, lifted a little or none above the sea-level.

Second. The action of the shore waves forming in great part the sandstone of the Potsdam, which in the southern end of the Hills is, in many places, composed at base of a thick bed of water-worn boulders or cobble-stones, that could only have been formed by the action of the waves on a shore line. Northward we have found nowhere this shore deposit, but, like the mass of the Potsdam elsewhere, it is a uniform coarse sandstone. There is no doubt, however, that large parts of this formation were derived from sources more remote than the Black Hills area itself.

Third. A depression of the land surface so as to form a sea in which the limestones of the Carboniferous, four hundred to five hundred feet in thickness, were formed mainly by organic agencies, and in the latter part of this era an oscillation, permitting the formation of the alternate shore and deep-sea deposits, sandstones and limestone of the series above the mass of the Carboniferous limestone.

Fourth. An elevation of the land, followed by a gradual deepening of the waters so as to permit the shallow-water deposits, the impure sandstone at the base of the Red Beds; a continued depression of the land permitting the deposit of the mid Red Bed limestone in deep water, and finally, a long period of shallow-water estuaries or lagoons, along the entire base of the Rocky Mountains, permitting the red clay sediments, and the formation of the gypsum. This gypsum is the product of the evaporation of saline water, the gypsum or sulphate of lime being deposited before the sea salt. These lagoons were periodically flooded by fresh sea water, thus maintaining the supply of the deposited salts. These same circumstances, excepting the deposition of gypsum, continued for a still further period, permitting the formation of the Jurassic series; and then succeeded,

EAST & WEST SECTION-BLACK HILLS.

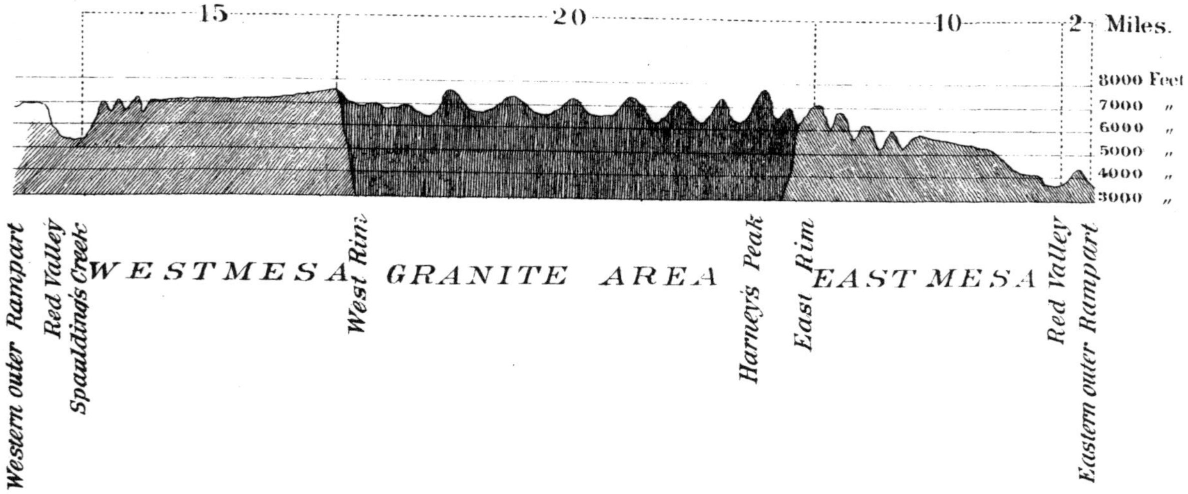

15 20 10 2 Miles.

8000 Feet
7000 "
6000 "
5000 "
4000 "
3000 "

Western outer Rampart
Red Valley
Spaulding's Creek
WEST MESA
West Rim
GRANITE AREA
Harney's Peak
East Rim
EAST MESA
Red Valley
Eastern outer Rampart

Fifth. A period of elevation succeeded by a gradual depression, during which the sandstones of the base of the Cretaceous were formed as a shore and shallow-water deposit.

Sixth. A continued depression of the land, a long period of shallow water, and the deposition of the clays and clay shales of the upper Cretaceous, while further south and southeast, in deeper water, were deposited at the same time the heavy limestone deposits of the Cretaceous, filled with marine fossils.

Seventh. Elevation of the mountains, as now constituted. This period in the sequence of events is of somewhat doubtful age, but, from the position occupied by the Cretaceous and other facts, I am constrained to place it as pre-Tertiary. The direction of the force producing the elevation, and the manner of its action, are questions I hardly dare, at present, to discuss, as they are subjects which even our ablest geologists consider still debatable ground.

The force was probably, however, propagated as a wave in an east and west direction, producing at the same time the main chain of the Rocky Mountains, to which system the Black Hills also properly belong. This force at various localities broke through the superincumbent strata, and in places was followed by an ejection of igneous matter. The maximum point of this outburst was undoubtedly near Harney's Peak, whereby the granites of that region were outpoured.

This granite is remarkably similar to the ejected granite of the entire Rocky Mountain range. The greatest action of igneous forces in the Rocky Mountains is stated by some observers to be from about the southern line of Dakota to Ccentral Colorado, which strip contains the peaks of greatest elevation in the entire range, this elevatory force dying out toward the south and north. So in the Black Hills we find the centers of igneous action in the north to be marked by less evidences of high heat and great force, as in many instances the strata around are little tilted and changed. To this class belong Terry's, Custer's, Inyan Kara, Bare, Warren's, Devil's Tower, and other peaks. That the elevation was not previous (as stated by Professor Winchell) to the deposition of the Red Beds is evidenced by the accompanying sketch through Crow Peak. At this peak the strata are physically unchanged, excepting the Potsdam sandstone, which is, for a considerable thickness, converted into a hard compact quartzite.

All the peaks above mentioned are composed of a feldspar porphyry very uniform in character. Upon the Red Beds, as shown in the section of Crow Peak, the Jurassic and Cretaceous beds are found to lie conformably, dipping with them, thus proving the post-Cretaceous age of the uplift and ejection of the igneous rocks.

Eighth. A large areal depression, followed by a

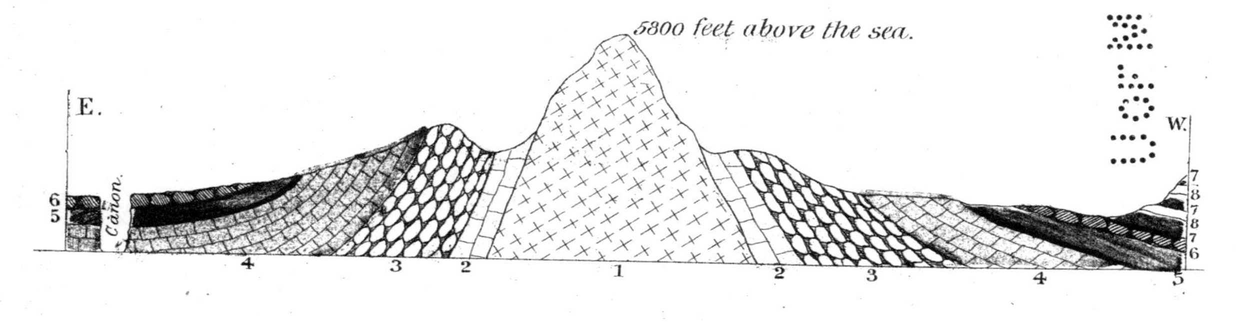

E.
W.
5800 feet above the sea.
Cañon.
7 Red clay
8
7 Red clay
8
7 Red clay
6 Purple Limestone
5 Red clay
4 Impure Sandstone
Red Beds.
3 Carboniferous Limestone.
2 Potsdam Sandstone, largely changed into quartzite.
1 Nucleus of feldspathic porphyry.

gradual elevation, permitting the shallow fresh-water deposits of the Tertiary, clays, etc., of whose extension, however, across the Hills in a continuous sheet we have no evidence whatever.

Ninth. A final elevation of the lands, over which probably there was spread a sheet of ice—the Glacial Period—the few evidences for which I have already mentioned.

Tenth. That there have been no great changes in the level of the Hills above the sea since the last great uplift, or rather that they have not been submitted to any great depression, is evidenced very strongly by the fact that there is nothing to show the former existence of a deeper system of drainage than the present one.

The immense denudation, however, since the close of the Tertiary, is evidence of the vast duration of time that must have since elapsed.

SURFACE.

The present result of the ages of force, whose action is described by Mr. Newton, is a huge pustule on the surface of the earth, with an enclosed core of granite, surrounded by a higher rim of secondary.

This rim is well defined throughout its whole circumference, and the ground falls or slopes away from it in both directions. On the inside the rains and frosts of ages have torn away projections, the higher portions falling down to fill up and smooth away the inequalities of the lower, until, at the present time, it is probable that some considerable portion of the original granitic area has been covered and hidden by washings from the overtopping secondary.

Although the whole of this part of the Hills is by this process much softened and rounded from its original asperities, the inside of the rim is still very abrupt in descent for some hundreds of feet. From the foot of the mésa, on the inside, the ground slopes toward the center very gradually until broken by granite ridges.

On the outside of the rim the general surface preserves its original level, with a slight slope from the rim, forming a great mésa or table-land, surrounding the whole central core, from five to thirty-five miles broad, and sinking suddenly to another level. On the southeast this mésa is so broad as to cross the south Cheyenne, which stream cuts its way through it in a deep and difficult cañon.

Taking their rise in the rim, the waters have cut in this mésa long slopes, tortuous channels, and magnificent cañons.

Surrounding this mésa on every side, and one of the most marked and peculiar features of the Black Hills, is a depression, which, from the color of the soil, was called the Red Valley.

This valley, well defined, but more or less broken by hills and ridges, is from one to fifteen miles in width.

On the outside of this valley, and a seeming outer rampart to the "sacred fastnesses" of the Black Hills, is a range of hills from four to eight hundred feet above the valley.

This range is generally narrow, but one or two hills in width. On the northeast, however, it widens out into an independent mass of mountains, attaining a maximum elevation of six thousand nine hundred feet, covering an area of at least five hundred square miles, and making the Black Hills consist of two distinct massės of mountains, separated by the Red Valley, here from five to fifteen miles wide.

This mountain mass has also a central granitic area, small and illy defined, however, as compared to the eastern section of the Hills.

From the foot of the outer rampart of the Hills the ground slopes away with more or less abruptness to the general level of the plains. A reference to the sectional drawings will show better than description the peculiar general characteristics of this remarkable country.

The central bowl-shaped depression constitutes the granitic area. Surrounding this on all sides is the great secondary mésa, highest on the inside, and gradually sloping away, to fall suddenly into the Red Valley. The "outer rampart" encloses the whole.

Nowhere have I traversed a country of equal area whose surface is so greatly diversified. There is no form in which Nature spreads, piles, or cuts her materials which is not repeated again and again in endless variety, within the narrow limits bounded by the two principal branches of the Cheyenne river. The granitic area is especially uneven. Granite ridges radiate from Harney's Peak as from a center. These are cut by other ridges, oblique or perpendicular, and, except the creek "bottoms," and a narrow belt along the base of the western Carboniferous "rim" (which has been somewhat smoothed over, as heretofore described), there is no level land in the granite region.

The mésas bounding the granite on north and south, though cut by numerous profound chasms, are yet by far the most level part of "The Hills." The upper portion is rounded by the action of the elements into long, gentle slopes. At a distance of from twenty to thirty miles from the interior rim, these mésas sink suddenly down into the Red Valley, giving rise to some magnificently broken and picturesque effects.

In the vicinity of Terry's Peak, the northern mésa is so torn by the action of water as to render the country almost unfit for the use of man. Just here the great eastern and northern secondary rims surrounding the granite, come together. In every direction diverge cañons, profound in depth, abrupt in declivity. To get through this country with wagons is a matter of fortunate accident, as well as of knowledge. Even on horseback, one becomes so entangled in thickets and cañons as to be forced to dismount, and sometimes to turn back.

The north face or wall of the north mésa is exceptionally high, steep, and broken. Through the immense mass of secondary, several huge granite cones have thrust their sharp heads, producing more or less disruption of strata, which the elements have not failed to take the utmost advantage of. Some of the grandest contrasts and most splendid effects of mountain and gorge are to be found along this face. The Red Valley, the great dry moat which surrounds the huge fortification of the Black Hills, is extremely irregular in surface. Sometimes it is really a smooth, beautiful valley, in other places it is a jumble of low, broken red hills cut by innumerable ravines, and looking like a Virginian "old field" on a large scale. The northwestern section of the "Black Hills" is even more broken than the principal division.

The appearance of the granitic area from the top of one of its prominent peaks is almost indescribable. One seems to be in the center of a great circle of rocks, hills, crags, mountains, valleys, ravines, and cañons, mixed and jumbled in intricate confusion, without system or order. The mountains seem to have been pushed up at haphazard; the cañons to cut them at will, in any and every conceivable direction. Generally, such a view would give some idea of the water-shed, but nothing can be gained from any study of this most disorderly mass of material.

The view on the opposite page is taken from the top of Harney's Peak, looking southeast across a country almost absolutely impassable. Wild and broken as the country appears in the picture, the photograph fails to do justice to the reality, bringing too near those crags which are near, or which are specially lighted up by the bright sun's rays, and throwing off too far those which are far, or which are in shadow.

The white crags which mark the brink of the abyss in the near foreground, apparently almost on a level, are actually more than a thousand feet below the position of the instrument, and standing on the rock from which this picture was taken, a man feels that with one vigorous bound he could reach the bottom of the abyss, more than two thousand feet below him.

SCENERY.

As might be imagined from the peculiarities of surface, there can scarcely be a country where the scenery is more varied. From the top of some lofty peak the explorer gazes in wonder at the infinite variety at his feet. Grand mountains, frowning crags, gloomy abysses, dense forests, and intricate jungles

FROM HARNEY'S PEAK LOOKING SOUTH-EAST.

alternate with lovely parks, smooth lawns, and gentle slopes. Each portion of the Hills has its own especial peculiarities of scenery. The tops of the grand mésas are lovely with long grass and flower-covered slopes, set as it were in frames of the dark green forests of pine. Lower down, the slopes become ravines, then cañons.

Nearly the whole surface of the mésas except the narrow "bottom" land of slopes and valleys, is covered with a dense growth of pine. As we leave the upper surface in either direction, we find in this forest openings, larger or smaller, sometimes several miles in extent and very irregular in shape. The surface and soil are apparently identical with that covered with timber, yet there is not a tree or shrub, nothing but a rich green carpet of grass. This is a "Park." These lovely openings add not a little to the beauty of the scenery.

Inside the granitic area, the scenery is truly fascinating in its loveliness. High and abrupt mountains, covered with dense dark forests, are suddenly succeeded by smooth grassy meads. An open park, extending apparently for miles, is abruptly terminated by an almost perpendicular chasm of four to eight hundred feet, its sides hidden from view by a dense jungle of pine, spruce, and quaking asp.

Huge bare rocks rise without warning from the smoothest plain. One struggles through dense, apparently interminable thickets, over masses of broken rocks, up and down steep ravines, to emerge at the most unexpected moment upon a smooth, well-kept flower-covered lawn, as varied and beautiful in form, and as perfect in finish, as was ever conceived by the most enthusiastic landscape-gardener. One finds himself continually saying, " what perfect taste," and at every turn in the varying landscape, he wonders that he does not find the elegant residence of the owner and deviser of all this beauty.

Only mountains and rocks, ravines, valleys, woods, and flowers go to make up the scenery, yet it never becomes monotonous. Though the materials be few and simple, the combinations are as varied as the figures of the kaleidoscope, and though a general sameness pervades the whole, each picture taken by the eye is a gem, differing from all others, and perfect in its every detail.

In the vicinity of the Harney group, the appearance of the rocks is varied, fanciful, and striking in the extreme. If a huge caldron, miles in extent, had been filled with molten granite, more and more heat applied until the whole was seething, bubbling, and flying up in the most violent commotion, and then at a word suddenly cooled in the very act of ebullition, no more irregular or extraordinary forms could have been assumed.

The tops are yet bare as when they were formed,

but the slow processes in the workshop of nature have been able in the lapse of ages to disintegrate a little, even of the solid granite, and the particles falling down have filled the crevices of the rocks themselves with sufficient soil to afford nourishment and support to that lover of rocks, the pine.

Every fissure is a nursery from which springs the dark green foliage, to hang lovingly around the gray old rocks, hiding their nakedness, giving life and animation to their stolidity, and changing their ugliness to beauty.

The view depicted on the opposite page is one of the most common forms of the scenery of the Harney group.

Entirely different in every respect is the scenery of the tops of the great mésas. That of the west has already been sufficiently described. It is tame, the country being a succession of undulations covered with dense thickets of pine timber.

That of the north and south mésas might also be regarded as tame, but for its simple beauty. There is nothing wild, or elegant, or grand. Except where the surface is bare rock, the level top of the mésa is always covered with pine. But the rains have necessarily made some impression on this upper surface.

Commencing at the very rim, the ground slopes away from the center in gentle depressions, from a few yards to a quarter of a mile in width, and in which for several miles there is scarcely a waterway.

For some reason, not easily ascertained, but presumably from the peculiarities of drainage, these depressions are bare of timber. Each such an one appears like a beautiful eastern meadow, carpeted with rich grass, ornamented with varied flowers, and bordered with trees—first a thicket of quaking asp, then higher up, the pine. The quaking asp is a deciduous tree, a species of cotton-wood, small but very straight and shapely. The foliage is a very rich light green, and contrasts prettily with the dark green of the pine.

Besides these natural openings there are also many larger ones, "parks," very irregular in shape, and dotted with rocks and clumps of timber. This portion of the "Hills" only lacks substantial farmhouses, magnificent barns, and frequent fences, to be very like some parts of the Cumberland Valley in Pennsylvania.

The eastern mésa seems to have been subjected to greater convulsion than the others. It is very greatly broken and disrupted, and though the general inclination is from the rim, as with the others, it appears, as it were, to have been crumpled and folded into a series of huge ridges, parallel to the general direction of the rim, and separated from each other by profound chasms.

The streams which rise inside the granitic area have forced their way through these opposing ridges by narrow cañons, deep and tortuous. The scenery possesses little variety, and but one element of grandeur. It it awe-inspiring. No one can look upward at the immense crags and narrow rift of sky, as seen from the bottom of one of these cañons, or downward from the top, into a chasm so narrow and so deep that the bottom is lost to view, without realizing his own insignificance as compared to the wonders and the powers of Nature.

The scenery of the north face of the great north mésa is the most striking and varied. From the Red Valley this face rises like a huge battlement, with grand towers at irregular intervals, the splendid granite peaks which rise through and above the general level.

The scenery of the Red Valley is very striking, but possesses a general sameness.

That most curious of the many curious features of the Black Hills, the " outer rampart," must, at some time in earth's history, have been a reef around the island now called the Black Hills. The Red Valley was a reservoir in which were collected the waters which flowed from the "Hills." These cut their way through the barrier, not necessarily on the natural prolongation of any stream, but wherever they found the easiest outlet. The cañons formed, though not remarkable for depth, are very regular and beautiful, their walls being formed of different shades of reddish sandstone.

The cut opposite represents the cañon by which Cold Spring Creek, one of the streams of the southern mésa, cuts it way through the "outer rampart." It is several miles in length and very tortuous. The walls are almost absolutely perpendicular, a remarkable fact, since the material of which they are formed, though a sandstone, is yet so soft that it can be cut by pick and spade. These walls are from three to six hundred feet in height, and of all shades, from light, delicate pink, to dark, rich red, the colors blending and intermingling in endless combination. The gorge averages scarcely more than two hundred feet in width, in many places narrowing to fifty feet.

The cut opposite the next page represents the same cañon near its upper end, and just before it debouches into the Red Valley, which is just beyond the high hill in the center of the picture.

This hill, though considerably higher than the other hills of the "outer rampart," is yet entirely composed of the same soft red or parti-colored sandstone, which, contrasting with the dark green of the pine, with which the hill is partially covered, renders it a very beautiful and striking landmark.

The scenery of the great northwestern section of the Hills, though very grand, is less varied than that of the principal section. There are no long, pine-

COLDSPRING CAÑON, W.T. IN RED BEDS.
Walls different shades of reddisd Sandstone.

dotted slopes, no mésas, and the gorges, though deep, are not cañons, their sides being more or less widely flared. The whole mass has the general shape of a huge cone, the hills toward the center constantly overtopping those on the outside, until the mass of hills culminates in the grand central cone, Warren's Peak, its top rising six thousand nine hundred feet above tide-water.

From any of the very high peaks in either section the view has the same quieting, depressing effect as a view of ocean. At our feet is the confused black mass of tumbled hills; around these, on all sides, is the limitless expanse of prairie, level and dead as ocean; while here and there, afar off, the face of a white cliff shows like a breaking wave.

SOIL.

The soil of the granitic area is a rich black loam, admirably adapted to agricultural purposes. This is true of almost every portion of valley or hill or mountain, on which there is any soil whatever. The glades in the forest, the park openings, the creek bottoms, the hill sides, are all covered with a thick carpet of splendid grass, such as is only grown on the richest soil. The soil on the tops of the mésas is somewhat lighter in color, but apparently equally good, the result, in grass and other luxuriant vegetation, being equally fine.

The Red Valley varies greatly in the quality of the soil of various localities. In some places it is filled with alkali to such an extent as to kill off all vegetation, except cactus and a scanty growth of thin grass; in other, and the greatly larger portions, it is covered with a rank growth of the very finest "gama" or "buffalo" grass.

The vicinity of Inyan Kara, in spite of the alkaline streams and red clay soil, is second, as a grazing ground, to no place in the Hills. Here, too, we found the creek bottoms filled with hops, as fine as I ever saw cultivated. Plums, gooseberries, and some few other wild fruits grow in great profusion.

As we get away from the vicinity of the Hills, the soil gradually deteriorates, until, near the south Cheyenne, or Belle Fourche, we find the ordinary soil of the plains.

There appears no reason why the Black Hills should not be a most magnificent agricultural country. Some portions will undoubtedly be so; in other portions, the season may prove too short for certain agricultural products.

However it may turn out as a farming country, there can be no doubt of its immense value as a grazing country. Splendid grass, pure water, excellent shelter from storms—nothing is wanting to fill all the requirements of a first-class stock-farm. It will, before many years, furnish beef and mutton, butter, cheese, and wool for a nation.

The country is not adapted for stock ranches of immense herds, water being so plentiful that they would stray, and the thickets being too dense for proper supervision of them. For farmers who own a few head of fine blooded stock, I think the Black Hills will be the Vermont of the West.

These remarks refer to the Hills proper. The Red Valley and the outlying plains country offer immense advantages to the large stock-owner. Hundreds of thousands of cattle and sheep can be subsisted and wintered on the foot-hills and contiguous plains.

THE CLIMATE.

The climate is sufficiently varied to suit the tastes of almost any person or class. We have no knowledge of the winter climate, except from the reports of the miners who built the stockade, and passed several months of last winter on French Creek. These unite in commendation. The winter was cold but clear, the temperature remarkably equable. There were no storms of any disagreeable magnitude, and the first serious snow-storm occurred just before they were brought out in March.

It is hardly fair to judge even of the spring and summer climate, by the experiences of a single year, more especially since we were almost continually moving, changing not only our position, but our altitude.

If, however, the experiences gained under such circumstances are to be regarded even as approximate tests, I can pronounce the climate of the Black Hills well-nigh perfect. Scarcely a day was too hot, scarcely a night so damp or cold that we could not sit out and enjoy ourselves around the camp-fire.

There is no such thing as a hot night. Though extremely susceptible to heat, I slept not a single night in the Hills under less than the equivalent of two blankets, and many times, even in midsummer, I required more.

I have already mentioned that on the 11th day of June we encountered, in the elevated gorge named by Custer "Floral Valley," a sharp snow-storm, alternating with sleet and rain. This valley is more than six thousand feet above tide-water.

On French Creek, at an elevation of fifty-eight hundred feet, we had a severe killing frost on the night of the 10th of August. There is abundant evidence that the season, in these very high altitudes, is too short for an agricultural country.

For five weeks, from 14th June to July 20th, Camp Harney on French Creek was the center of operations of our exploring and surveying parties. We had therefore a much better knowledge of its climate than of any other portion of the Hills. It is five thousand six hundred and twenty feet above tide-water.

The climate is superb. Though it sometimes felt

hot by day, and damp and cold by night, the thermometer was never above seventy-eight degrees, nor below fifty-four degrees. A series of observations (not so regular as might be wished) gave a mean temperature of sixty-two degrees, and a daily variation of fourteen degrees. A few similar observations at Camp Crook, on Rapid Creek, in the latter part of July, resulted in a mean temperature of sixty-four degrees, with a daily variation of twenty degrees. On the 24th of July, on Rapid Creek, a severe hail-storm sent the mercury from eighty-four to sixty-two degrees, twenty-two dègrees in half an hour. Camp Crook is at least a thousand feet lower in altitude than Camp Harney.

The rain-fall in the Hills proper, seems to be sufficient. Showers were very frequent, and we had some regular storms, during which the rain came down in a steady pour for all day, and even for two days.

The following are the dates on which we had rain; the steady pours are marked ×:

May 25, 26, 29,

June 1, 9, 11, {snow sleet rain}, 13, 17, 18×, 22, 25, 26, and 30×,

July 4, 5, 9×, 10, 12, 13, 16×,17, 20, 21, 22, 24, 25, 26, 30, 31.

August 7, 12, 14, 15, 19, 24, 25, 26×, 27×, 30.

September 1, 8 ×, 9 ×, 12, 30.
October 4, 5, 6.

From June 4th to September 15th, we were either in the mountains, or so close as to have the same climate.

Thunder-storms are quite frequent, terrific in force and power, and fearful in the vividness—the nearness of the lightning. They are often accompanied by wind, and sometimes by hail. Scarcely a day occurs in summer, that there is not a thunder-storm in some part of the hills.

One afternoon, from the top of one of the high mountains near Harney's Peak, I saw five separate and distinct storms, occurring at the same instant in different parts of the Hills. One of these struck a portion of our party with very nearly fatal results, three persons and several horses having been prostrated by one lightning-flash. Most fortunately only one horse was killed, though two of the persons struck were seriously injured; one, the young son of an officer of the expedition, did not entirely recover for some months. The lightning in this case acted most curiously: A heavy rain-storm coming on, two soldiers and the boy took refuge under a tall pine. All three were seated on a rock about six feet from the trunk of the tree, and each held in his hand the reins of his horse's bridle. At the flash the three persons and horses were thrown to the ground, one of the soldiers

DEVIL'S TOWER, DISTANT VIEW.

being pitched quite a distance, alighting on his head. The surgeon was promptly on hand. Each person had been struck on the cheek bone, just under the eye. The fluid passed down the person of each, going out at the ball of the foot, boring a hole in the shoe-sole as clean and round as if made by a bullet, and raising a large blood-blister on the bottom of the foot. All were bruised under the eye and blistered on the foot. Neither had any other mark whatever.

Skipping from the men to the horses, the flash prostrated all, striking each just over the eye. Two soon recovered their feet, the third, the farthest from the tree, was killed. This bolt came down the pine tree, cutting a deep groove in the bark, and entering the ground with the roots of the tree, yet, on its way down, it parted with sufficient of its power and destructive force to do the damage described.

During this storm, which lasted scarce half an hour, more than twenty trees were struck by lightning within a radius of a few hundred yards. Another curious, and to me unaccountable phenomenon, attended this and the other storms of the same day. I have said I was on a high mountain of the Harney group. At least three of these storms were, in different directions, within four miles of me in a direct line, the clouds being, probably, five hundred or a thousand feet below me. Though I could see the vivid and incessant flashes of lightning, not a sound of the thunder could be heard. Every one of the party with me noticed this very remarkable fact, and we all spoke of, and tried to account for it. None of the explanations were or are satisfactory, and I present the fact to the scientific world in the hope that a satisfactory solution of the problem may be arrived at.

Throughout the Hills the number of trees which bear the marks of the thunderbolt is very remarkable, and the strongest proof of the violence and frequent recurrence of these storms. The electric current acts in the most eccentric way. In some cases it will have struck the very top of a lofty pine, and passed down, cutting a straight and narrow groove in the bark, without any apparent ill effect on the tree, which remains green and flourishing. At other times the tree will be riven into a thousand pieces, as if with the blows of a giant axe, and the fragments scattered a hundred feet around. The woods are frequently set on fire and vast damage done. There are many broad belts of country covered with the tall straight trunks of what was only a short time before a splendid forest of trees, now charred, dead, and useless. The largest of these fires occurred on the head waters of Box-elder Creek. What was evidently a beautiful body of timber fifteen miles long by at least five broad, is now only dead trunks, some standing, but by far the larger portion prostrate, lying in every conceivable direction on and across each other, and making travel through them a trial sufficient to test the skill, patience, and Christian forbearance of any explorer, more especially as the standing trunks, partially decayed, are swayed with every breeze, and seem "just tottering to a fall."

The "park" country already spoken of is almost wholly due to fires. A forest is destroyed. In a few years another fire destroys the young growth which may have sprung up. This happening several times at intervals of a few years, effectually destroys both roots and seeds, and converts pine forests into parks.

As if to neutralize to the explorer the effect of the fierce and vivid lightning, the rainbow of the Black Hills is a marvel of perfection and beauty. Two or three times wider than the rainbow of the States, it forms a complete and perfect arch, both ends being sometimes visible to the beholder, and one so near and distinct that there would be little difficulty in locating that traditional "pot of gold." Unfortunately the bow is only a "bow of promise" with reference to water.

Very frequently the rainbow is doubled, and several times I saw three distinct arches, the third and higher being, however, a comparatively faint reflex of the brilliant colors of the lower.

That curse of the plains, wind-storms, are not of

frequent occurrence in the Hills proper. The thunder-storms are sometimes preceded or accompanied by a violent gust which, however, is soon over, Old Æolus apparently contenting himself with one vigorous blast. Though we had in the whole summer no practical and unpleasant experiences of their power, we yet had ample proof of how vigorous these blasts can be, in swaths of uprooted trees, in broken branches, and wrenched-off tops. Owing to the broken, irregular nature of the ground, and the number of high points of hills and mountains, these tornadoes, however violent, do but little damage. They cannot sweep for miles over the surface, destroying everything in their path, as such storms often do in the middle and western States, but are broken into eddies, turned and twisted through the hills and over the gorges, touching only here and there, and soon expend their force and power.

In the wider portion of the Red Valley, which is only a slice of plains sandwiched between the two great masses of the "Black Hills," these tornadoes have full sway, and are very destructive. The edge of one touched a portion of our camp one afternoon. This edge was so sharply defined, that though our mess-tent, in which we were taking dinner, received a rough but not noteworthy shake, the hospital tent not a hundred yards away was completely wrecked in an instant, and the "red beds" rendered more nauseous by the outpouring of a large quantity of jalaps and salts, and other compounds with which doctors shorten our lives. The doctor himself was, I believe, the only mourner over this calamity, and I am afraid that our quartermaster positively rejoiced, as he was saved the further transportation of a great quantity of totally useless stuff.

The character of the flora indicates that the climate of the belt of country just at the outside foot of the great mésa, is much milder and more "eastern" than that of the granitic area. This is especially the case on the north and east faces. We passed through this section in the autumn. Even as late as the 1st of October, the country was still beautiful; the grass was scarcely browned; autumn flowers bloomed in profusion; deciduous trees still were green, or were just beginning to show "the sere and yellow leaf."

The frequent thunder-storms is the only flaw in the otherwise perfect Hills climate. There were, troops and miners, more than a thousand persons in the Hills last summer. They were scattered from one end to the other, throughout every portion. There were also several thousands of horses and mules.

The case given was the single instance of any person or animal being injured by lightning. A little precaution in keeping away from tall, prominent trees, is all that is necessary for safety, even in the most violent storm.

STREAMS.

Every stream of the principal section of the Black Hills takes its rise either on the inside or on the outside of the high Carboniferous rim which surrounds the granitic area. This rim attains its greatest height on the northwest. Here, on a broad mésa, whose top is almost a level, stands a solitary rock forty or fifty feet in height above its base. The top of this rock is the most elevated point of the Black Hills, being seven thousand six hundred feet above tide-water. There are but five streams which carry water out of this section of the Hills, and it is a singular coincidence that each and every one of these streams takes its rise in the sides or near vicinity of the grand mésa on which stands this rock, to which our surveyors gave the name "Crook's Monument," in honor of the commander of the military department of the Platte. This singular landmark is not visible from the outside of the Hills, being covered by the long slope of the mésa, but from every vantage-ground on the inside it appears unique and unmistakable.

All the streams which rise in the south rim flow to the southward. The rains have cut the surface of the south mésa into long, beautiful, grass-covered slopes, which, gradually deepening, become at last deep, narrow, and crooked cañons.

The country is covered with pine timber, in which are many irregular "park" openings.

Lith: by Kimmel & Voigt. N.Y.

CROOK'S MONUMENT, HIGHEST POINT OF BLACK HILLS.
alt: 7600 feet.

Though there are occasional springs, not one of these cañons has continuous running water, and this, to the eye, most perfect portion of the Hills, may turn out to be less valuable than it appears, simply from a lack of a sufficiency of that prime necessity.

Only two of these south-flowing streams are worthy of special mention. Many deep and narrow "box" cañons (cañons with perpendicular rocky sides, permitting no lateral ingress or egress) unite to form a wide and deep gorge, perfectly dry until it reaches the foot-hills.

Suddenly a fine large stream, carrying quite two thousand miners' inches, springs from the bottom of the gorge, and, after a course of only twelve miles, joins the South Cheyenne river.

This stream is called by the Indians Minne-catta, or Warm Water Creek, the temperature of the water where it bursts from the ground being seventy-four degrees Fahrenheit, entirely too warm for drinking purposes. The Minne-catta is also remarkable for a fine cascade, the water rushing in an almost unbroken sheet over a precipice fifty feet high.

The other curious stream our surveyors named "Amphibious" Creek, from the fact that its bed is about half the time dry, and the other half a nice running stream. Bursting from the ground in springs, the water runs for a mile or two, then sinks as suddenly as it came. After an underground course of a mile or two, it again springs to the surface. This is continued for the whole length of the stream, and that it is the natural and permanent condition is proven by the fact that, wherever the water is above ground, it contains numerous fish.

Five streams flow to the eastward, all taking their rise on the interior or eastern slope of the great western mésa. After a short course in the comparatively level country at the base of this mésa, they plunge into the deep and dark chasms which they have cut for themselves through the opposing granite ridges. The most easterly of these ridges is parallel to and directly in contact with the interior of the eastern secondary rim, making a mountain mass of parallel ridges, one or more primary, the others secondary.

So long as these streams are in the primary or granite they continue to gain in force and volume, but as soon as they get into the crumpled folds of the dislocated secondary, they disappear entirely (with one exception, Rapid Creek).

FRENCH CREEK,

three hundred miners' inches, is the most southerly of these streams.

Rising in the southwestern rim, and flowing for fifteen or twenty miles through a most beautiful country, it plunges into a deep and tortuous cañon,

CAÑON OF FRENCH CREEK, D. T.
1200 feet deep 30 feet wide at narrowest.

from which, near twenty miles below, it emerges as a dry bed. The cañon is so difficult, that only a single person succeeded in getting through its whole length. He accomplished the feat on foot, and in the face of difficulties which would have deterred any but the most persistent. He came out utterly exhausted, unable to take but a few steps without resting, but he has the proud satisfaction of knowing that he has been where no man ever was before. At one place the cañon is scarce thirty feet in width, bounded on each side by sheer walls of solid rock, not less than twelve hundred feet in height.

It is impossible for pen or pencil to convey an idea of the realities of such a scene. The view opposite, though true to nature, fails to impress the mind with that sense of awe which a sight of the gloomy obscurity of this awful gash in nature's bosom cannot fail to awaken.

Of all the streams of the Black Hills, French Creek is most like home to us. Camp Harney, on its banks, was our abiding-place for nearly six weeks, and no one of our party was so callous as to leave it without regret.

Of all the streams, it waters the country most grateful to the eye. The valley above the cañon is most lovely, a series of parks, long reaches of the richest sward, covering hill, valley, and ravine. At irregular intervals, huge rocks thrust their heads through the green turf, and clustered about each such mass, as if offspring of the granite, is a group of pines, towering to the skies. On each side the valley is shut in by hills, their sides covered and their summits crowned with dark forests of pine.

Camp Harney is a most lovely spot; a level sward of thick turf surrounded by low hills and bare masses of granite. The soil of the valley is a deep rich loam, to all appearance as fine for agricultural purposes as any I have ever seen anywhere. The grass is magnificent, and is set so deeply, and its roots so completely matted, that our horses, though tied to the same picket lines for near six weeks, did not with their hoofs cut through the sod.

The country, well watered and covered with grass even to the very top of the mountains, is admirably adapted to stock-raising.

The timber on French Creek is more abundant and of better quality than elsewhere in the Hills.

We found many miners on French Creek, all very enthusiastic on their "gold prospects." More work was done on this creek during the summer than on any other, and, if the miners are to be believed, with very satisfactory results.

On August 10th, French Creek was almost dry, the water standing in holes. The grass was parched and burned, the leaves on some of the trees were already changing color. On the night of that date we were visited with a severe killing frost, proving very conclusively the shortness of the season.

The free use of the water for sluices, etc., by the miners, had, undoubtedly, something to do with its dryness, for Custer, at the same season only a year before, found this a beautiful running brook.

SPRING CREEK,

seven hundred miners' inches, is formed by the junction of a great number of lovely brooks all taking their rise in the western rim. The country drained by it is much more broken than that drained by French, and it has to pass by deep and narrow cañons through no less than three mountain ranges, in the last of which it disappears. The valley is lower than that of French.

The valley is narrow, the mountains on the southeast towering to very great heights. A range of abrupt hills on the other side sends rocky spurs towards the mountains, forcing the creek into continual curves and narrow cañons.

In crossing the heads of Spring Creek one passes through a constant succession of parks and forests, over divides, and across or along valleys. The country is remarkable for its varied and picturesque beauty, for the fertility of the soil of its valleys, and for its forests of pine. As a grazing country it cannot be surpassed, and the only doubt as to its value as an agricultural country, is suggested by the shortness of the season.

Following down through the first deep cañons to where some of these tributaries have united, we find Spring Creek carrying about three hundred inches of water.

Still further on, Spring Creek cuts its way through a second granite range, in cañons remarkable for their singular beauty. Still increasing in volume, it plunges into the cañons cut in the great east mésa, and is lost. With a fine deep bed, it yet carries no water out of the Hills.

The timber in the gorges of the lateral tributaries of Spring Creek is in some places very fine, though nowhere so good as that on French Creek.

The amount of arable land is not great, the mountains and hills encroaching too closely on the valleys.

Gold was found in very considerable quantities, and Mr. Jenney thought this the best mining stream of the Hills.

There is ample water for sluices, and there is no doubt but that the gold on this creek will richly pay the hydraulic miner.

It is a lovely dairy country, full of beautiful sites for residences, timber and building-stone being convenient and abundant, and everywhere is the most ample supply of cold, pure water.

RAPID CREEK,

two thousand miners' inches, is the largest of the streams which flow east, and the only one which, escaping the thirsty secondary, pours out upon the plains an undiminished volume.

Several creeks unite to form it; the most important of which was named Castle Creek by Custer. The gold-diggings in Castle Creek are regarded by the miners as the best in the Hills.

Rapid is a very beautiful stream of pure, cool water, flowing with great velocity over a pebbly bed of twenty to thirty feet in width. For twenty-five miles of its course it flows through a tortuous cañon, so deep that the sun's rays strike directly into it for scarce an hour of the day; so narrow that in the whole twenty-five miles there is scarcely an acre of arable land to be found in a body; so difficult that a horseman can only get through with the greatest labor, and even then he must lead his horse much of the way. The sides of this cañon are almost everywhere covered with dense forests of small pine and spruce; the bottom is a jungle of quaking asp, willow, and other bushes, bound and matted together with vines in great variety. About a mile above Camp Crook the creek suddenly emerges from all these obstacles, the bottom widens out into a grassy mead of half a mile, the hills fall back, and, from pine-covered, abrupt declivities, become long, steep slopes, park openings and open pine forests alternating in picturesque beauty. This continues for about two miles, when the creek, as if tired of the sunlight, plunges again into a dark chasm, filled with an almost impenetrable jungle, and from which it only escapes when it has nearly passed out of the Hills. The valley is not a valley. It is simply a tortuous gorge, a thousand feet below the general level of the country on each side. The soil is good, but there is little of it. There is good grass in the opening near Camp Crook, scarcely any on the sides or in the bottom of the cañon. Back from the creek two or three miles, on the heads of the tributary brakes and cañons, there is fine grass. The country, though not to be compared as a grazing ground with French or Spring Creeks, will nevertheless support considerable herds of stock. The timber is generally poor, a very small percentage being fit for sawing, and that most difficult to get out. Rapid offers, within the Hills, but little to the agriculturist. It is, however, a fine mill-stream. Very few miners have been on this creek, bnt the "prospects" are very fine, better than on any other stream.

About two miles before Rapid Creek leaves the Hills, the deep cañon in which it has been flowing widens out into a beautiful valley two miles in width. It is one of the loveliest and most valuable valleys of this country. The sides and summits of the hills are covered with forests of pine timber better than the average. The gorges at their bases are filled with oak, ash, elm, box-elder, birch, and other deciduous trees. The soil of the bottom is rich loam, covered with the finest grass. The water is pure and excellent, and the stream amply large for saw-mills. The climate and flora are as "eastern" as any other place in the Hills.

It is one of the very choicest spots in the Hills for the settler. Unfortunately there is gold enough in the sands and soil of the creek bottom to induce some Vandal to put the whole of it through sluice-boxes, leaving the now lovely valley a desert of rocks and sand. The country is well watered, there being numerous small pure streams. There is abundant timber for building purposes, fencing, and fuel, and unlimited limestone for building or other purposes.

Even on the plain Rapid continues to be a beautiful stream, but after getting six or eight miles from the Hills it loses its purity, becoming murky and discolored, though the water remains excellent to the taste. It also becomes less rapid, having long reaches of comparatively still water, separated from each other by series of rapids. There are also numerous beaver-dams. The bed is more or less filled with aquatic plants, and becomes a fine feeding-ground for numerous wild fowl. There is very little timber or brush of any kind on the creek, after its escape from the Hills, until it reaches this stage, but from here to its junction with the Cheyenne there is very considerable cotton-wood and willow. The soil of the "bottom" is excellent, and fine grass covers "bottom" and adjoining hills. The uplands are ordinary broken prairie for about twenty-five miles from the Hills, where the creek enters the "Bad Lands" formation. After this there are no beaver-dams, the "bottom" gets narrower, the bordering hills more abrupt; the tertiary soil washed from these renders the creek bed boggy and very difficult to cross. The timber grows very much larger, thicker, and better. The trees, October 3d, are almost as green as in spring. The water becomes somewhat alkaline after reaching the tertiary deposits, but is not unpalatable or injurious. The streams which unite to form the Rapid have lovely "bottoms" of rich soil covered with the finest grass. This portion of the Black Hills is the most perfectly watered country I have ever seen. Every little valley has a lovely brooklet, and from the sides of the Hills thousands of springs pour their stores of pure, sparkling, cold, and delicious water. Nowhere have I seen water so naturally cold. Even in midsummer their temperature was almost that of ice-water, being generally forty-one or forty-two degrees, Fahrenheit. One spring near Castle Creek showed thirty-nine degrees by actual test. All these streams have very considerable arable land along their banks, and this will be a splendid country for the settler. There is also a fair growth of pine, and an unlimited supply of the finest building-stone.

From source to mouth, Rapid Creek is a fine stream, and all things considered, probably the most valuable in the Hills.

BOX ELDER,

three hundred miners' inches, drains a large area, it having numerous branches of splendid water. The country drained is one of the most beautiful and valuable of the Hills.

Its general level is at least five hundred feet above Rapid. It has innumerable beautiful valleys, and large bodies of arable land. The soil is very rich, and is everywhere covered with magnificent grass. There is comparatively little timber; the forests on its numerous heads having been killed within a very few years by fires.

Gold was found on this stream, but not in considerable quantity.

The cañon cut by this creek is one of the most striking. It is wider than most of the others, and the " bottom " continues for quite half through the mountain mass.

The stream makes a desperate effort to escape the secondary, and get out on to the plain, and almost succeeds, losing itself only six miles from the Red Valley.

Custer's trail comes down this creek on his return trip.

ELK,

three hundred miners' inches. The heads of this creek have many lovely valleys of splendid soil covered with the richest grass, but they are narrow, and there is no great quantity of arable land.

Beavers have dammed all these streams, converting the valleys in many places into bogs, covered with dense jungle.

There is a very fair growth of pine on the "divides" between the streams.

"Color" was found in the washings of this creek, but though it rises in the granite, its course is almost entirely in the secondary, and but little gold is likely to be found on it.

There is an abundance of splendid building-stone, and as this is undoubtedly a good grazing country, it offers considerable attraction to dairy farmers.

These five are the only streams which rise within the granitic area.

On the northeastern slope of the great northern mésa several streams take their rise, the most important of which is

BARE PEAK CREEK,

which drains the country about Terry's Peak, to the south and east. Its heads are innumerable, every gorge and cañon having running water, none of which, however, flows out of the Hills.

These gorges are of immense depth, twelve to fifteen hundred feet, and are separated from each other by narrow ridges and back-bones, sometimes so very narrow and the sides so steep as to make a horseback ride along them a test of nerve. These hill-sides are thickly covered with pine timber, some of that low down being quite good.

There are no "bottoms" to the gorges, nor an acre of arable land in all this section. There is no grass. The country is unfit for the use of man, and entirely useless except for its timber, which however, will scarcely pay for the trouble and expense of getting it out.

I have already said that there are but five streams which carry water out of the Hills. These are Rapid, Spear-fish, Red Water, Inyan Kara, and Spaulding's Creeks. The first only rises in the granitic area, the others on the outside of the rim. The heads of all intermingle or are contiguous, and cluster about a common center, Crook's Monument.

The finest of these streams is the

RED WATER.

This is a splendid stream, the finest of the Black

Hills. It is from thirty to fifty feet wide, by an average of twenty inches deep. The water is pure, and clear as crystal, and, the fall being nearly a hundred feet to the mile, the current is tremendous.

This, being the largest, and the type of the streams running northward through the great secondary mésa, is worthy a special and minute description.

Many long slopes deepen into gorges, and unite to form what Custer named "Floral Valley," one of the principal branches of Red Water.

For from three to six miles from the summits of these slopes the gorges are dry. Springs there appear, and a brooklet flows through each valley for a mile or two, and disappears.

Less than a mile below the point where these gorges unite, the whole valley breaks out in springs, sending a splendid mill-stream from an acre of ground.

This is the true head of Red Water. The valley gradually deepens. The stream, meandering from side to side, gradually grows smaller and smaller, until at about fifteen miles from its splendid source, the water entirely disappears. Still the valley grows deeper, and narrows into a gorge, the sides become precipices, and about fifteen miles below where the water disappeared, it has become an immense cañon, with almost perpendicular sides of fifteen hundred feet, the bottom impassable even for a horseman.

No one of our party succeeded in getting through this cañon. It is believed, however, to be fifteen or twenty miles long. The bottom is filled with rocks and fallen trees and a jungle of underbrush, and, so far as known, has not a drop of water. About three miles from where the stream emerges from the cañon, the water rises again from innumerable large springs, and these uniting in a few yards, form the beautiful river which flows in undiminished volume to the Belle Fourche.

SPEAR-FISH CREEK.

This creek is only second in volume to Red Water, being about three-fourths its size. It is purer, colder, clearer, softer, deeper, and much more rapid, rushing between its banks with the force of a cataract. It differs from all the other streams which flow north through the mésa, in that it does not sink anywhere. Rising with a bound from the earth, not far from Crook's Monument, it flows with the directness and force of a torrent, eating away its rocky bed until it has cut a cañon for many miles of its course of not less than two thousand feet in depth. One of the surveying parties, getting into this cañon from its head, found not a single place for more than thirty miles where its walls could have been scaled, and had to force a way through to where it comes out on the northern plain.

After emerging from this gorge, it has a "bottom" of over a mile in width. This is well timbered with ash, elm, oak, and box-elder, many of the trees being quite two feet in diameter. We are now nearly on the level of the outside plains, and the climate is much softer, plums and grapes abundant, and the flora altogether "eastern." The soil is the finest I have seen, a deep, rich loam, and the whole valley is a splendid meadow, on which fine hay could be cut (September 15th). It is the finest agricultural valley yet found, and the grazing is superb. There is pine in the gorges of the mésa to the south, and splendid building-stone on the side hills.

About seven miles from the north opening of the gorge which it has cut in the mésa, this creek joins the Red Water. United they form a stream well worthy the name of river. The bed is about fifty feet wide, and the water, averaging nearly three feet in depth, rushes with great and very uniform velocity between its banks. These are about six feet high, evenly rounded, and covered with grass to the water's edge, leaving no beach or bare spot, and appearing like the well-kept banks of an artificial canal. There is no timber or brush of any kind on this part of the creek. The "bottom" will average a mile in width, is perfectly level, and covered with the richest growth of grass and a great variety of flowers. To the north is a belt of high red hills, running east and west, and on which is some dwarf pine. Numerous streams come in from the adjoining slopes and hills, on all of which is a thin belt of timber, cotton-wood, ash, elm, box-elder, and white birch.

INYAN KARA CREEK,

two hundred miners' inches. The principal branch of this stream rises within rifle-shot of the head springs of Floral Valley (Red Water). The country drained is immense for so insignificant a stream. Rising partly in the great north mésa, and partly in Red Valley, where it is widest, this stream has peculiar characteristics. I have already described the high, carboniferous limestone mésa, cut by the action of water, at first into long, gentle, grassy slopes, gradually deepening into valleys, with sides rounded and covered with pine. As soon as these have deepened until the limestone is cut through, the water appears, springs everywhere pouring their pure and sparkling stores from the seams between the limestone and the mass of red sandstone which underlies it, and uniting in the valley. Still the valley deepens. In a few miles, sometimes one or two, sometimes fifteen or twenty, the red sandstone is cut through, and the brook disappears in the thirsty strata beneath. The valley now narrows to a gorge, and finally cuts its way by a deep and precipitous cañon to the plain, where it appears as an insignificant arroyo, a scarcely noticeable gully, either dry or so impregnated with all nauseous tastes, acquired in the red bed and gypsum formation, as to be unfit for the use of man. Hundreds of lovely valleys such as described, each, at some period of its course, graced by a beautiful brook of pure water, unite to form the miserable little alkaline stream, "Inyan Kara Creek." Nowhere have I ever seen so bountiful a provision of beautiful valleys, rich in grass and sparkling with streams, go to make so poor a result. The whole country is covered with the richest gama grass, and as these alkaline streams are even preferred by cattle, this region will some time support thousands.

Curiously enough, there are, even in the red-bed region near Inyan Kara, many springs of pure water, which seem to come from crevices in the limestone. For drinking, the water must be taken from the very head spring, as but a short course in the red bed and gypsum-filled soil is sufficient to render it unpalatable.

There is not a great deal of arable land on this creek, the "bottoms" being narrow. What there is, is very superior, producing not only the finest grass, but wild fruits and berries in great variety and abundance. Plums, grapes, gooseberries, buffalo berries, and a curious raspberry which grows on a stalk between two broad leaves. It is sometimes called button-berry.

All these fruits, except the grape, are very sweet, juicy, and palatable. The grape is the frost or winter grape, very small and tart.

In many of the little "bottoms," the bushes are almost completely covered and bound together by a thick growth of hops, as fine in all respects as I ever saw cultivated in the best hop regions of the States. In other places, the red washings from the Hills supported a thick growth of wild rye, from four to five feet high.

There is no timber on the lower Inyan Kara Creek, except a scanty growth of cotton-wood ; the neighboring mountains, however, have sufficient pine for all purposes of the settler. Everywhere on this creek is an ample supply of most excellent building-stone.

No gold was found on this or any other of the streams of the great north mésa. About half way between Red Water and Spear-fish Creeks, in a country entirely carboniferous, we came upon a great number of small quartz stones scattered at random over the ground.

This caused a considerable flutter among our miners, who called it "float quartz," and said that it indicated the presence of gold at no great distance.

Indications of gold were also found about the great isolated granite peaks of the north face.

SPAULDING'S CREEK.

This is the middle or principal branch of Beaver Creek. Its head springs are scarce a hundred yards from those of Inyan Kara. It drains a considerable country, but the water, except at the head, is not good. Our route into the Hills led up this creek, and a full description has already been given. There is no gold on this creek or on any of its tributaries.

BELLE FOURCHE.

For four or five miles below its junction with Spear-fish Creek, the Red Water keeps a generally north course, receiving three tributaries from the southwest and west.

The last or farthest north of these issues from a narrow gorge in the red bed. It is a miserable little alkaline stream, a thin sheet of water, ten feet wide by some three inches in depth, and of a milky appearance. Up to its junction with this insignificant apparent tributary, the Red Water has retained the characteristics already mentioned, being deep, rather narrow for the water carried, very swift, with frequent deep holes, and low, grassy banks. The moment it receives this little stream from the west it changes not only its course, but its whole character; turns to the eastward, spreads into a wide channel with numerous bars, and is nowhere more than two or three feet deep. The country becomes more broken, the banks of the streams high and abrupt, and lined with trees and bushes. The little stream is the Belle Fourche, though we could not make up our minds to believe it for several days. This stream has scarce any bottom land. It has cut for itself a gorge from fifty to one hundred feet deep, in the high table-land, and turns and twists in it, having everywhere a high bluff bank on one side or the other.

There is no soil that can be cultivated, no timber but cotton-wood; the country is worthless, except for grazing, being covered, for some miles below its junction with the Red Water, with splendid gama grass. It will support immense herds of stock.

As we go down, the stream gradually diminishes in volume, becomes wide and shallow, the water more and more alkaline and nauseous. The stones and rocks in its bottom are covered with a yellowish-white, slimy deposit.

The grass is less and less good, and the country, below the mouth of Bare Peak Creek, becomes barren and valueless, an ordinary alkaline plain in appearance and qualities.

SOUTH CHEYENNE.

Where we crossed this stream the last time, just above the mouth of Spring Creek, it carries about two thousand miners' inches of water, clear and pure to the eye, but so impregnated with alkalies as to be unpalatable. This is spread in shallow rills over a sandy bed four hundred yards in width.

In many places the banks are scarcely perceptible, the grass-covered sand of the bottoms on either side merging gradually into the sand of the bed. The stream is full of quicksands, and can be crossed in only one or two places in many miles. The "bottom" averages about one mile wide, the bordering hills being several hundred feet high, and very abrupt. The soil is generally of the poorest quality. There are, in the "bottom," a few rich spots covered with fine grass, but most of it is sand or washings from the tertiary hills. Grass covers even this apology for soil, but it is thin and poor. There is a considerable irregular growth of cotton-wood along the streams, some of the trees being very large, and a few small sycamores (or button-wood trees) struggle for a precarious existence in the edge of the sandy bed. The grass on the hill-sides, and on the top of the great tertiary mésa, is very much better than that in the bottom, and the country, poor and uninviting as it is, will yet support numerous herds of cattle.

There is no timber or stone suitable for building purposes.

I have elsewhere stated that the northwestern section of the Hills is a huge mass of mountains rising cone-like to the center. Numerous streams start from the sides of this central cone, and diverge, joining either the Belle Fourche, Red Water, or Inyan Kara.

Near their sources these streams are all pure, good water, but almost all soon become impregnated with alkalies, though to a very different extent. Thus, one branch of Sun-dance Creek is fairly good water, another more nauseous and horrible than a whole apothecary shop.

The whole Black Hills country is profusely watered. Almost everywhere, even on the very tops of the mésa (with the few exceptions already given), there are fine springs, giving birth to lovely little brooks. These sink before arriving at the Red Valley. This valley is splendidly watered on the north and east, pure delicious springs rising in the most unexpected places. On the south and west the water is more scarce, and is moreover generally very bad, being impregnated with the impurities of the red beds.

It is a singular fact, for so well watered, broken, and Alpine a country, that there is not a single lake in the Hills proper, and only two small ones in the whole country between the Cheyenne and Belle Fourche. These are in the Red Valley, between Red Water and Spear-fish Creeks. The largest is near half a mile long by two hundred yards wide. It is almost entirely surrounded by a marsh covered with tall tula grass, making the total dimensions nearly double those given. They are fed by underground springs of pure water, and though no stream enters either, a very pretty little brook flows from each. Thousands of water-fowl sported on the waters, always, however, at a most exasperating distance from the banks.

MOUNTAINS.

As already stated, the very highest ground in the whole Black Hills country is on the northwest Carboniferous rim. This is not a mountain, though it rises to the height of seven thousand six hundred feet above tide-water, but simply the inner edge of the great north mésa, which everywhere in this vicinity has the same general level. "Crook's Monument" is a huge castellated rock, rising like a tower above this general level.

Within the granitic area the country is so broken, and the mountains are generally so nearly of equal height, that, except the Harney group, no one peak asserts itself over the others.

The Harney group consists of seven immense peaks rising from one grand base, no one being more than two hundred feet higher than the others.

The two most northerly of these peaks are about three miles apart, and connected by a curtain of al-

THE FINGERS, HARNEY'S RANGE LOOKING NORTH EAST.

most bare rock, scored and fissured by the action of the elements, and plunging with almost precipitous abruptness nearly two thousand feet into the gorges at the base. The eastern mountain is Harney's Peak. The western was named by the surveyors Dodge's Peak. In an almost direct southeast line with Harney, three other grand peaks rise to almost equal height; and in an equally direct southwest line from Dodge, are two other similar peaks.

Harney's Peak owes its prominence to an immense crown of granite, not only raising its head above the other peaks, but rendering it, from the north, east, and west, the most remarkable and notable landmark in the Hills. It is visible and distinguishable at immense distances on the prairie to the northeast.

The view of Harney from the south is obstructed by an immense fringe of bare rocks, rising near enough to an equal height to shut out that mountain. To this curious fringe our surveyors gave the name "The Fingers," from some fancied resemblance to up-pointed fingers of many hands. (See cut on opposite page.)

Our surveyors succeeded by the aid of ropes and long poles in scaling the crown, "Tower Rock," of Harney's Peak, and from this position were enabled to obtain an unobstructed view of the whole area of the Hills, and to locate with great accuracy the direction of all prominent points.

This being done from many of the notably prominent peaks of the Hills, the accurate position of each was determined by triangulation.

Harney's Peak is seven thousand four hundred and forty feet above tide-water. The other six peaks of the same group are from one to two hundred feet lower.

TERRY'S PEAK

is the next in height and prominence, attaining an elevation above tide-water of seven thousand two hundred feet. It is an immense mass of granite, which has been thrust up through the secondary strata of the great north mésa, producing the most extraordinary and complicated disruptions, and rendering its vicinity the most broken portion of the Hills. It is an immense and splendid mountain, and is visible from almost every portion of the Hills, while, from the northern prairie, it is the most prominent landmark.

CUSTER'S PEAK

is just in the edge of the northern carboniferous rim, and for some time was supposed by our scientific corps to be a detached portion of the great mésa. A more minute examination disclosed the fact that it also has a central core of granite, though it is so surrounded and overlaid with secondary, as scarcely to be discoverable. It is a very symmetrical, well-formed mountain, rising to the height of six thousand seven hundred and fifty feet above tide-water.

CROW PEAK,

a huge granite cone, rises through the secondary, just on the north face. It is very striking and prominent. Around its base is the largest body of oak timber to be found in the Hills—the higher growth of oak intermingling with the lower growth of pine. It is the only place in the whole country where I found the two trees growing together. Crow Peak is six thousand two hundred feet high.

Several other granite cones of less prominence rise through the secondary, but are scarcely worthy a special description.

WARREN'S PEAK.

The great brown peak which is the culmination of the conical mass of mountains constituting the north-western section of the Black Hills, was, by our surveyors, named Warren's Peak, in honor of General Warren, of the United States Engineers, whose route near the base of this mass, in 1854, is the first recorded survey of this country.

Rising mountain upon mountain, peak after peak, to a common center, this is the most imposing mass of mountains in the Hills, though its top is seven hundred feet lower than Crook's Monument.

The mountain mass of which it is the center is called the "Bear Lodge Range." It is six thousand nine hundred feet above tide-water.

On some of the streams which take their rise in its sides, gold was found in great abundance. The miners who explored this granite area, found it small in extent, but very rich.

INYAN KARA.

Rising from the western edge of the Red Valley is a splendid mountain with a granite cone, rising six thousand seven hundred feet above tide. Warren translates the name, "The peak that makes the mountain." "Inyan" means mountain in some of the Sioux dialects, but my interpreter was unable to translate the word "Kara."

BARE PEAK

is a most prominent landmark, being visible for many miles in every direction.

On preceding maps this mountain has been called Bear Butte, and the creek which flows by its base, Bear Butte Creek. This is so evidently a misnomer that our surveyors changed the name to what the original namer evidently intended. The elevation is a cone of solid granite rock, entirely devoid of all vegetation. "Butte" means an elevation too high to be called a hill, too low to be called a mountain. This peak rises to the height of five thousand two hundred

Lith: by Kimmel & Voigt. N.Y.

BARE PEAK FROM MOUTH OF BARE PEAK CREEK.

feet above tide-water, and, standing on the plain several miles from the nearest mountains, appears yet higher. It is not a "butte." "Bare Peak" expresses exactly what it is, and that name was accordingly bestowed upon it by our surveyors.

The sketch opposite gives an admirable view of this peak, as seen from near the mouth of Bare Peak Creek, about fifteen miles off in an air line.

DEVIL'S TOWER.

On the north side of the Belle Fourche, not far from the mouth of Inyan Kara Creek, in a country very broken, but the general surface of which is comparatively level, rises one of the most remarkable peaks in this or any country.

An immense obelisk of granite, eight hundred and sixty-seven feet at base, two hundred and ninety-seven feet at top, rises one thousand one hundred and twenty-seven feet above its base, and five thousand one hundred feet above tide-water.

Its summit is inaccessible to anything without wings. The sides are fluted and scored by the action of the elements, and immense blocks of granite, split off from the column by frost, are piled in huge, irregular mounds about its base.

The Indians call this shaft "The Bad God's Tower," a name adopted, with proper modification, by our surveyors.

The following table of elevations will give an idea of the general variation of level of the different portions of country included between the Belle Fourche and South Cheyenne rivers:

Crook's Monument	7,600	feet above tide.
Harney's Peak	7,440	" "
Dodge's Peak	7,300	" "
Four contiguous peaks	7,200	" "
Terry's Peak	7,200	" "
Warren's Peak	6,900	" "
Custer's Peak	6,750	" "
Inyan Kara	6,700	" "
Crow Peak	6,200	" ".
Transfer Valley	6,100	" "
Camp Harney / French Creek	5,600	" "
Camp Terry	5,550	" "
Bare Peak	5,200	" "
Camp Bradley	5,200	" "
Devil's Tower	5,100	" "
Camp Jenney	5,000	" "
Camp Crook / Rapid Creek	4,700	" "
First crossing of S. Cheyenne	3,000	" "
Mouth of Rapid Creek	2,500	" "
Camp Raynolds, on Belle Fourche	2,500	" "
Junction of South Cheyenne and Belle Fourche	2,375	" "

Many portions of the Black Hills are exceedingly

Alpine in appearance and character, but the peculiarities of formation, as shown in the sectional drawings opposite page 45, detract from the grandeur of the *coup d'œil.* The position of a mountain with reference to its surroundings has everything to do with its apparent height. Thus, Crook's Monument, the very highest point of the Hills, makes no show, because in a region the whole of which is extremely elevated. We encamped many times in lovely flower-covered valleys, which are higher above the sea-level than the rock-crowned summit of Crow Peak.

Looked at from near Camp Transfer, across the wastes of the Red Valley, Inyan Kara seemed to loom almost to the skies, yet its top was only six hundred feet above us.

Bare Peak, rising from the comparatively level plain, appears the highest mountain of the Hills; yet its summit is more than two thousand feet below the general level of the great north mésa.

RED VALLEY.

I have already described this valley as coinciding for some miles with the valley of Spaulding's Creek. When that creek goes into cañon, the valley passes to the westward over high rolling ground, and widens out to several miles.

This portion of the Black Hills is simply a slice of plains sandwiched between mountains. It has the regular plains climate — everything at extremes. When hot, it is very hot; its cold is very cold; its rains are deluges; its winds are tornadoes. The surface is very broken, much cut up by ravines. Many of the small hillocks or divides between these ravines are wrapped, as it were, in a thin shell of limestone, which conforms to the undulations and inequalities of the hill itself.

The creeks have very little bottom land, the ground rising first into a sort of upland valley, then into long slopes and mésas. Every portion of these valleys, slopes, and mésas, where rocks do not prevent its growth, is covered with a thick sward of the richest "gama" or "buffalo" grass. The little "bottoms" in the bends of the creeks are filled with small ash, box-elder, and plum, which are many times almost completely hidden by a thick mat of hop-vines.

On the east stretches a range of high mountains, many of them cut by rains into almost perfect cones, and all clothed to the summits with pine. On the west is Inyan Kara, the culminating peak of a range of mountains which, commencing at Camp Jenney, runs in a generally northern direction, widening as it progresses towards the Belle Fourche, and forming a distinct and separate portion of the Black Hills, the northwestern section.

That portion of the Red Valley lying just at the

base of the north mésa will, in my opinion, prove to be the finest agricultural portion of the Black Hills. It is barely three thousand feet above tide-water; the climate is mild; the trees in great variety—oak, elm, ash, box-elder, and some cotton-wood; not any very large growth of either, but sufficient to indicate the great difference between this and the climate inside the Hills.

The flora is very like that of western North Carolina. The soil of the creek bottoms is a very rich loam, with grass in some places several feet high.

On the east side of the Hills the Red Valley is generally very narrow. The water which sinks in the deep secondary cañons rises to the surface in this valley in the most unexpected places, in springs, to be swallowed up in a few miles by the thirsty prairie.

The climate is much warmer than that of the Hills. Oak and birch grow in the gorges, and the flora is very "eastern." The soil of the valleys is very rich, and the whole country is covered with splendid grass. The Hills proper, only a few miles west, are covered with pine timber, and the immediate vicinity has an unlimited supply of limestone, much of it already cut by stratification into convenient blocks for building purposes. It is a splendid country for the settler, and will support untold herds of cattle.

On the southeast, south, and southwest the Red

Valley is generally narrow, dry, and sterile. The grass is poor, and the little water alkaline.

There is nothing to tempt either the agriculturist or the stock-breeder, and, besides being of all the Black Hills country the most obnoxious to the explorer, this portion offers the least inducement to the settler.

TIMBER.

Much has been said of the timber of the Black Hills, as one of the principal sources of its future wealth. For one hundred miles from north to south, by fifty from east to west, the country is more or less thickly covered with pine timber. After days and weeks of travel over dreary, monotonous, treeless plains, it is very easy to become enthusiastic over trees of any kind. It is not, therefore, unnatural or to be wondered at that such a splendid body of timber should cause the explorer to over-estimate the quality and quantity of the "lumber" to be obtained from it.

The very large mass of these pine forests, dark and rich and beautiful as they are, are yet composed of trees the very large majority of which are less than eight inches in diameter. There is scarcely to be found in the Black Hills a forest of old trees. Large, fine saw-logs are to be found, and in very considerable numbers, but rarely in large bodies. Scattered through the young forests are old and large trees which by some means escaped the fires that de-

stroyed others of their age. Occasionally, in the "bottoms" of creeks, or in narrow gorges of the mountains, will be found some acres of really fine timber, suitable for merchantable lumber. The finest of these forests is in the "bottom" of French Creek, some miles below the miners' stockade. For several miles along the creek, a strip of an average of a hundred yards wide is covered with pine trees of great size, two to three feet in diameter, and in many cases forty or fifty feet without a limb. The situation being admirably protected from winds, the trunks are remarkably straight and free from cracks and flaws.

The south mésa is fairly covered with a body of pine of very uniform size and appearance, eight to twelve inches in diameter. The branches grow low, however, and a tree is rarely found which would yield over twenty feet fit for the saw-mill.

The high ground on both sides of the northern rim is very densely covered with pine and spruce, generally small, scarcely averaging eight inches, and with the branches growing almost to the ground.

The immense plateau of the west mésa is very densely covered with thickets of pine, very small, averaging scarcely six inches, but from the very thick growth they are very tall, and are without branches for thirty, forty, or even fifty feet. These trees are just the right size for railroad ties, and this forest will furnish enough for all the roads which are likely to be constructed within a reasonable distance in the next hundred years.

These poles are also admirably suitable for building small log houses, barns, cribs, etc.; and scattered through the smaller growth are larger trees sufficient to furnish the boards necessary for floors, doors, etc.

The Bear Lodge Range is not so well covered with pine as the eastern section of the Hills, and it is generally rather small, with branches almost to the ground. In the gorges there is, however, some fine timber, sufficient for all purposes of the settlers. This portion of the Black Hills will, in my opinion, only support a scanty population.

I estimate that there are, in the two sections, something over four thousand square miles of country more or less covered with pine. Of this, including the Red Valley, the parks, the bare bottoms and valleys of creeks, I estimate that four-tenths are entirely without timber. Another four-tenths is composed of young forests, excellent for railroad ties, small buildings, fencing, etc., but not yet fit for the saw-mill. One-tenth is wind-shaken, or injured by lightning or fire, and one-tenth is good lumber. In other words, I think that this four thousand square miles will furnish not more than one-tenth of the merchantable lumber that would be obtained from an equal area of the virgin pine forests of

Michigan or North Carolina. There is an abundance of lumber for all purposes of the country itself, but, except ties, it will not furnish any very large quantity for exportation.

In many of the gorges there is a fine growth of spruce, some over two feet in diameter, and not less than one hundred feet in height. These tall trees attract the lightning, however, and many of them have been killed.

On the northern and eastern faces of the Hills, there is a scanty growth of oak, ash, elm, box-elder, and white birch. The oak is a white oak, of sometimes a straight fiber, like the basket oak of the Eastern States. Generally, however, it is dwarfed, knotty, crooked, injured by fire, and fit only for posts and fire-wood.

On Spear-fish Creek the ash and elm are sufficient for fencing; elsewhere there is hardly enough for fire-wood.

Everywhere in the Hills is found more or less quaking asp. This, though a beautiful ornamental tree, is small, soft, soon decays, and is fit for nothing except that when dry it makes a tolerable fire-wood.

Willow and cotton-wood are also found in considerable quantity on the dry beds of the streams outside the Hills.

None of these woods can be counted on as or for "lumber."

GOLD.

The granitic area of the eastern section of the Black Hills is an irregular ellipse of about forty by twenty miles on its longest diameters, and contains about seven hundred square miles. In every portion of this area are indications of the presence of gold, except just under the great western rim, where, as has been already stated, some portion of the original granite area has been covered up by washings from the overtopping secondary.

In the valleys of the streams gold is found almost everywhere, in the bars, in the gravel and sand of the beds, even in the "grass roots." Every stream within the area yielded gold, but I saw no single spot where the quantity obtained would pay the ordinary pan miner.

The "pans" varied from a mere "color" to eight or ten cents in value.

I heard of a pan which yielded twenty-seven cents in fine gold scales. I personally saw no pan washed out which yielded more than about ten cents. Occasionally a small "nugget" was found. The largest I saw weighed ninety-six cents.

French Spring and Rapid Creeks yielded about alike. Castle Creek, the principal tributary of Rapid, was the favorite among the miners, but Mr. Jenney preferred Spring.

The gold of Castle Creek is coarser, and what the miners term "rusty," being discolored in some way, some of it being quite black. This adds to the care necessary in its separation from the sand and dirt. A novice would lose much of it, as he would never take the black or dull-looking apparent pebble to be a valuable "nugget" of the "real stuff." There is sufficient gold on each of these creeks to pay well the ground-sluice and hydraulic miner.

French Creek has a small body of water with little fall. It can never be thoroughly mined. Spring Creek is larger, and has fall enough to make the mining effective and easy, while Rapid Creek has so much water, and so great a fall, that the whole valley, and much of the hill-sides, can be put through the sluice-boxes.

Pan mining will pay nowhere in the Hills. Sluice and hydraulic mining will pay on French Creek; it will pay well on Spring Creek, and best on Rapid Creek.

Box-Elder and Elk Creeks have so short a course in the granite, that though there is gold on each, it is to be doubted if in any great quantity.

The Hills are full of rotten quartz veins, leads as favorable in appearance as any I have ever seen. In the vicinity of Camp Harney, these veins are parallel to each other, and pursue a course almost due north and south. They are from one to five hundred yards apart, and cover an extent of country several miles in width. Their south ends start in the south rim, their north ends are lost in the granite mass of the Harney group of mountains.

On Spring Creek, Mr. Jenney discovered a mammoth lead, not less than one thousand feet in width, composed of innumerable smaller and parallel veins.

We had no means of testing the richness of these leads, but if they contain gold or silver in paying quantities, the value of the Hills is incalculable. The very number and width of these veins would seem to indicate that they contain little or no gold. Nature is more chary of her wealth. Appearances are, however, so favorable, that it is hard to believe that the Black Hills will not yet furnish its "Big Bonanza."

The granitic area of the Bear Lodge Range is quite small, containing altogether not over one hundred or one hundred and fifty square miles. This area is also very illy defined. The granite central core of this mass of mountains is closely covered and enveloped by the secondary, and it is only where it has been laid bare by the action of the elements, that prospecting has been possible. The miners who explored this section give most glowing accounts of the richness of the bars and placer diggings along the streams, and the favorable appearance of the quartz veins.

There is no doubt of the existence of gold in

greater or less quantities in every portion of the granite of both sections.

It is for the skillful or lucky miner to develop the quantity and position of this wealth. Our means were only adapted to the development of the fact of its existence.

I saw in the possession of a miner some good specimens of silver ore, which he said he had found in the hills between French and Spring Creeks. He claimed that he had discovered a splendid lead which would pay enormously.

Our party found no silver, and, as it is to the interests of the miners to make their claims as rich as possible, his story may be taken "*cum grano.*"

The mineral wealth of the Black Hills will, in my opinion, come from the development of the leads.

The valleys will confer wealth, not so much through the gold in them, as from their agricultural and stock-breeding qualities.

Fortunately, from lack of water, but two or at most three of these lovely valleys are likely to be turned into barren deserts of rock and sand.

MINERS.

Of each twenty men who will rush to the Black Hills as miners, nineteen would have been better off if they had remained at home. I am aware that this statement will deter no man from going, as the American people are so constituted that each man expects himself to be the twentieth.

There is a fascination in the search after gold not to be accounted for, and, for a dollar's worth of the shining precious grains, a man will devote patience and labor which would have brought him three times the amount of money in almost any other business.

Each newly-arrived individual (whether novice or old miner) has a feverish hope, almost an expectation, that he will be the fortunate finder of a "pot-hole," which will make his fortune in a day or two, and he works with a force and determination which deserves a better fate than it usually meets. After a few days his muscles tire, his energetic will relaxes, and, if disappointed, as he generally is, the average miner is content thenceforward to sit by and see some newcomer open his claim.

After it had been fairly demonstrated that pan mining in the Hills would not pay, there were, on French and Spring Creeks, last summer at least ten idlers for every working man.

With the persons who come really to mine, come also whisky-sellers, professional gamblers, and all those who live on the vices and passions of mankind. The idlers soon get to drinking and gambling. Some lose all their money. Ruined, wretched, and reckless, these organize into bands, which roam about the country, "jumping" the claims of persons who are defenseless, and are supposed to have a few dollars to pay for immunity.

Disappointment, idleness, and want, well armed and desperate, stalk through the land, stealing when opportunity serves, or taking, where they can do so with impunity.

All this was seen in the Black Hills last summer, and that murder was not added, was only because the miners were sent out of the country before many of the panderers to vice had arrived.

It has passed into a proverb that "placer" mining is the poor man's diggings, while "quartz" mining is only for the rich. Placer mining in the Black Hills will not pay the poor man unless he be a "Heathen Chinee." He may make a little money by securing a claim, selling it out to a man or company who has capital to buy up many claims; then looking for and securing another claim with the same intention and result.

This is a poor and precarious foundation on which to base a living. No man can make more than the barest wages by pan-working a single claim in the Black Hills. The "placer" mines, as well as the "quartz" mines, are here only for the rich man, and I would advise no poor man to go into the Hills with the expectation of making money by mining for himself. Of course he may be fortunate enough to strike rich "diggins" and do well; but, as a rule, he will make more money as day laborer for some wealthy man or company than he possibly can by working for himself on a single claim.

The reports of the enormous wealth of the placer mines in the Black Hills are the most bare-faced fabrications, got up by miners who wish to sell their claims.

The splendid specimens of gold-bearing quartz, advertised as on show in Sioux City and elsewhere, may be to be seen, but did not, in my opinion, come from the Black Hills.

Money is to be made here by men who have sufficient capital to buy up many claims along a creek, sufficient to warrant the expense of dams, ditches, and all works necessary for hydraulic mining. If they have already the means of comfortable livelihood, poor men had better stay at home, unless prepared to work on wages.

All this is said on the supposition that the Black Hills will, sooner or later, be opened to the miner. Under present circumstances, in addition to the disadvantages mentioned, he is liable at any moment to be arrested by the troops and sent from the Hills a prisoner.

Under the peculiar working of the complications of the present management of affairs, this arrest amounts to nothing except the annoyance and loss of time.

The military have orders to arrest and send out under guard every man found in the Hills. However distasteful such an order may be, it is obeyed, of course. But the military have no power of detention longer than the arrival of the prisoner at the nearest military post, from whence it is required that he be turned over to the civil authorities.

Curiously enough, that respect and obedience to law and orders, which is so marked a feature of our military establishment, seems totally wanting in the "Civil Authorities." The prisoners, violators of the law, turned over to them, are immediately released, without even bail for future good behavior.

An interloping miner is captured by the troops, sent a prisoner to the nearest military post, and from thence turned over to the civil authorities. Although more than a hundred men have thus been captured and sent out, not one has in any way been punished or even detained by the civil authority. They are at once set at liberty, and immediately start again for the Hills.

One man stated, "I have been captured and sent out from the Hills four times, besides coming out voluntarily under Crook's proclamation. I give the troops more trouble in catching me each time, and I guess I can stand it as long as they can."

As an evidence of the well-disposed, law-abiding disposition of the average American citizen at all times, and under all circumstances, I think it but just to speak of the action of the crowd of miners who were in the Black Hills last summer.

By the 20th of July the Hills were swarming with people. At least six hundred men, evading the guards set around, had already gained access to the Hills, and were engaged in prospecting and mining, many of them with hope of the best returns. General Crook, having orders to send them out, himself came into the Hills, mingled and freely conversed with these men, and finally decided upon his plan of action. A proclamation, kind but decided, was issued. The miners were required to leave, but were requested to do so voluntarily, and a miners' meeting was recommended on the 10th of August, prior to their departure.

The effect was remarkable. The generous policy, the kind but firm manner, backed by a few well-chosen words, did effectually in a few days what it would have taken a heavy body of troops months of time, indefatigable labor, and enormous expense to accomplish indifferently.

I was present at the miners' meeting at Custer City, August 10th.

Here was a most motley collection of citizens of all ages and conditions of manhood, voluntarily relinquishing the bright anticipations and promises of wealth, cheerful, and if not contented, willingly acquiescing in the execution of an obnoxious law.

Here were men with bottles and vials of the precious grains, as evidence of their success in mining, leaving rich prospects, and, in their opinion, sure pecuniary independence.

Far outnumbering the scanty force of troops, completely armed, inured to all the hardships and dangers of the frontier, they would have been no despicable enemy to encounter even in pitched fight, on open ground; while, dispersed in the almost inaccessible fastnesses of the mountains, they might successfully have defied or evaded all the troops which might then have been sent against them; yet here they were, assembled in obedience to a proclamation, quiet and orderly, and going out without trouble or expense; not that they wished to or were obliged to, but simply because they had been kindly notified that their presence in the Hills was in violation of the law.

Never have I seen a body of men which gave me a grander idea of the inherent value and true worth of American men, and American institutions.

On the evening of August 10th, the beautiful valley of French Creek, near Custer City, was picturesque with miners' camps. At sunrise on the morning of the 11th, not a man or animal was to be seen.

The valley, so lately bustling with life, was still and solitary. Thin wreaths of smoke, arising from expiring camp-fires, were all that remained to tell of the swarm of people which crowded the valley only the day before.

A word or two of friendly warning to those who have made up their minds to "tempt the fickle Goddess," to try the various chances and changes, the hardships, privations, labors, and excitements of a miner's life.

To those whose fortunes are already at lowest ebb, I can give no advice. If no change can be for the worse, any change may be for the better.

Beware of the men who advertise as Colonel this or Captain that, to take out a great company, for a certain price each. They are generally the most remorseless liars and the most egregious swindlers. They will pocket your money, give you miserable food, worse sleeping accommodations, and make you walk all the way.

Six or eight neighbors and friends, who know and can rely on each other, should make up a party. Such a sized party can carry all their outfit and tools in one good wagon, drawn by a pair of stout horses or mules. If necessary, for mutual protection against Indians, several such parties may unite for the journey into the Hills, but on arrival each party should keep together, locate together, and work together.

Such a party is strong enough to deter loafing idlers from any attempt to "jump" their claims, yet few enough to require only one cook, who can also take care of camp while the others are at work. Those men who are necessarily obliged to go into the mining districts alone, should unite themselves with some reliable party as soon as possible. Each will necessarily have to pay a great deal more for his share of the provisions, etc., than he would had he belonged to the party when they were purchased.

Parties who go by their own wagons should purchase their outfit as far east as possible. Take an ample stock of provisions, a sufficiency of tools, bedding, and ammunition, but no luxuries, except vegetables and some canned food.

Work earnestly and faithfully, and when you have made up your mind that your venture at mining is a failure, either leave the Hills at once or select a good piece of land and locate as a permanent settler.

During the winter of 1874-75 a party of miners, consisting of twenty-two men and one woman, made their way into the Hills (by Custer's coming-out trail), and after devious wanderings finally located on French Creek, at the point named on the map Camp Harney.

Naturally, their first idea was safety, and ignorant of the characteristics of the Indians surrounding the Hills, they proceeded to build themselves a fortress.

The structure erected is a stockade work, eighty feet square, with flanking projections at the corners. The walls are of upright logs, set two feet in the ground and rising twelve or fourteen feet above it. These palisades are about ten inches in diameter, very straight, and set as close together as possible. The walls, as well as flanking projections, are loop-holed for riflemen, and the interstices between the upright logs are covered by battens on the inside.

There is but one entrance, and that on a side difficult of approach on account of the creek, and it is barred by a heavy bullet-proof double gate, and defended by loop-holes on each side.

The work is very defensible, and constructed with commendable skill and judgment, the more so as the builders were, in all probability, entirely ignorant of all rules of military engineering. But three mistakes were made. The defensive loop-holes are on the same level inside and out. A wily enemy, creeping up under cover of darkness, might have obtained possession of these holes, and slaughtered the defenders without danger to themselves.

The loop-holes should have been out of the reach of persons outside. An elevated platform, running around the entire inside, would have enabled the defenders conveniently to get at holes, entirely beyond the reach of an enemy. The same result might have

MINER'S STOCKADE, FRENCH CREEK.
80 feet square.

been arrived at by digging an outside ditch close around the whole work.

The battens protecting the narrow spaces between the logs should have been on the outside. A bullet, striking an outside batten, would probably be deflected into a log, and stopped; striking an inside batten it would be deflected, but it would still continue its dangerous course across the inside area.

There is no arrangement for barbette (or top) defense and watchfulness, a very serious omission.

As completed, the defenders cannot see the approach and position of an enemy except by looking through a narrow loop-hole, which necessarily commands a restricted view, and while the enemy is left to develop his plans comparatively unmolested, the defenders can only act after those plans are put in execution.

Defensible as the stockade undoubtedly is, it would have been in great danger of capture had it been on the plains.

Inside the stockade are five very comfortable log cabins, set on three sides of a court-yard. Between these cabins and the stockade wall was sufficient space for their wagons, animals, tools, etc.

These miners had also laid out a town, and the foundations of several houses were commenced.

This "town" will be a failure, as the town of

'Custer City," four miles above, is in much the best position.

This party was brought out of the Hills by troops, about March 1st, 1875. It had been located on French Creek only about four months, and the amount of labor performed by these twenty-two men was simply wonderful. Not only were the stockade and cabins built, but the whole valley was riddled with "prospect" holes, and far in the Hills, in every direction, quartz leads had been opened to greater or less depth.

They had not yet commenced regular mining, though some considerable gold was taken from the numerous "prospect holes."

Before the miners went out under General Crook's proclamation, they had already found time, in the intervals of their mining labors, to attend to that great first duty of all frontier American citizens, viz.: lay out a town.

A beautiful site was selected in the valley of French Creek, surrounded on all sides by lovely parks or pine-covered, craggy hills.

Its position is admirable, the best in the Hills, as, from the nature of the country, every north and south road through the eastern section of the Hills must pass through it, as does also the east and west road to Camp Jenney.

Every man in this particular "mining district"

was interested in this town. A commission was appointed, streets laid off and named, lots surveyed and numbered, and all went "merry as a marriage bell," until, all else having been done, it came to naming the town itself. This was of sufficient importance to call a general meeting of the persons interested. The miners were nearly equally divided into Northerners and Southerners. The Northerners decided to call the new town "Custer City," in honor of the commander of the expeditionary force which had first passed through the Hills. The southerners were a unit on "Stonewall" as the proper name. Debate ran high, and from words the opposing factions very nearly came to blows, rifles and pistols being freely brandished. Better councils finally prevailed, and it was determined to leave the question to the decision of that great arbiter of American quarrels, the ballot. A vote was taken. It was very close, the excitement ran high, and culminated in uproarious shouts of the Northerners, when the judges of the election finally arose and pronounced the name of the town "Custer City."

The ownership of the lots in the new town was decided by lot, each man drawing from a box a folded ticket, on which was written the number and block of the lot of which he thus became owner.

When the miners left the Hills, Custer City boasted

two large log structures, one of which was a court-house, the other intended for a hotel.

Two other "towns" were laid out in the Hills by miners last summer. One on Spring Creek, at the junction with the main road, off the road which leads to Castle Creek. The other on Rapid Creek, near Camp Crook. Neither arrived at the dignity of a house, and though each has an excellent site, and good position with reference to possible roads, I cannot recommend the purchase of the lots of either as a first-class investment.

ANIMALS.

I have already spoken in the most favorable terms of this country, as eminently fitted for stock-raising.

So far as one may judge from appearance, this is so, but there is still one doubt. Some portions of the Black Hills have less game, less animal life, than any wild country I have ever seen, equally suited to the tastes and habits of game, and this scarcity may argue something in climate or conditions unfavorable to its propagation.

Certain portions of the Hills we found teeming with animal life, other portions, equally beautiful and apparently equally well-fitted for game, was almost entirely without it.

Another very curious feature is the extraordinary

number of barren does, even in those portions of country where deer are most plenty.

Of sixteen does killed by myself, between August 15th and September 10th, only two had given birth to fawns this season.

I attribute the scarcity of game on French Creek to the presence of the miners at the stockade all winter.

The game had never been hunted or obliged to protect itself against human enemies. It knew nothing of its danger, and was easily bagged whenever encountered.

These men were dependent entirely on game for their fresh meat, and soon killed off the deer in the vicinity of their location.

The presence of these men will not, however, account for the scarcity of animal life in other places.

The great south mésa, that, to the eye, most perfect portion of the Hills, is especially bare, not only of game, but of animal life of any kind.

For so wild and beautiful a country, it is the barest of life I have ever traveled through. A hawk silently sailing far above the mountain tops; a few little chipmunks, a pair or two of snow-birds, or a busy, diminutive sap-sucker, is all the life to be expected from a six hours' ride through the beautiful parks and forests, hills and glades, south of French Creek.

Animals, birds, fish, and reptiles are in comparatively little variety, and not in very great numbers anywhere in the Hills. In a few localities, not differing in any external appearance from the general country, we found great numbers of deer. A very great many, probably a thousand deer, were killed by our party in the Hills, but I think I am safe in asserting that I have seen more deer in Texas, in one day, than I saw in the whole of my three months in this apparently perfect game country.

On Spring Creek we found a great many deer, though the miners were rapidly exterminating them.

Castle and the other tributaries of Rapid Creek abounded in deer, while on the main Rapid itself there are very few.

On the heads of Box-Elder we found deer in very great numbers, and in the broken country on each side of the great northern rim, bear, elk, and black-tailed deer were found in very considerable numbers. Bears are quite numerous throughout the Hills, the country being peculiarly adapted to their tastes and habits. Several varieties are represented, from the huge and dangerous grizzly, to the small and timid black.

Except one fish (which I am told is also found in the Laramie River), I saw no animal, bird, fish, reptile, or insect, which I had not seen before.

The animals of the Black Hills are:

Bears—grizzly, brown, and black; numerous.

Cougar—(mountain lion); a few.

Lynx—a few.

Wolves—large timber; numerous.

Foxes—silver gray; numerous.

Elk—not abundant.

Mountain sheep—A few.

Black-tailed deer—in considerable numbers.

Red deer—more abundant than any other animal.

Beaver—very numerous.

Squirrel—red pine; a few.

Woodchuck—ground hog; few.

Chipmunk—very small variety; abundant.

Mouse—numerous.

Some of the hunters reported that they had seen a buffalo. I, however, saw no tracks or other buffalo sign in the Hills. There are many old trails, showing that at one time this country was a favorite resort of the buffalo, but I am of opinion that the animal is now practically extinct in all this region.

BIRDS.

Considering the beauty of the country, the purity of the water, the density of the thickets, and the variety and abundance of insect life, there are very few birds in the Hills.

The ruff grouse (the New York partridge) is the only game bird in the Hills proper, though on the high west mésa, at an elevation of seven thousand four hundred feet above tide-water, I found a splendid pack of sharp-tailed grouse. This was undoubtedly exceptional, as none were seen elsewhere in the Hills proper. In the Red Valley there are great numbers of the sharp-tailed grouse, and packs of the sage grouse are occasionally encountered.

These and the little blue northern snow-bird are probably the only birds which are indigenous, though a very considerable variety come here to breed.

The following are the birds found in the Hills proper:

Black eagle.

Sand-hill or whooping crane—breed in the Hills.

Turkey Buzzard. Hawk—several large, and two or three small varieties. Owls—several varieties. Ravens. These birds are not abundant.

Mallard ducks—sheldrakes—very abundant; breed in and about the beaver dams.

Ruff grouse—not abundant.

Lewis and Clarke's woodpecker.

Red-headed woodpecker.

Yellow-hammer—(Flicker).

Kingfisher.

Sap-sucker—in three or four varieties; one very small.

Robin.

Blackbird.

Cow-bird.

House Martin—build nests in holes made by themselves in dead pine trees.

Barn-swallow—build in clefts of rocks.

Sparrow.

Snow-bird—the small blue eastern.

Goat-sucker, or night-hawk.

Kingbird—several varieties.

Bluebird.

Yellow-bird.

Dove.

Field-lark.

Sandpiper—very small.

Buffalo-bird—a large species of jay.

In the Red Valley are also found

Sage grouse.

Sharp-tailed grouse.

Bobolink.

Cat-bird.

Brown thrush.

Heron.

In the fall, all the streams and ponds, both inside and outside of the Hills, are alive with myriads of migratory water-fowl, geese, brandt, ducks, etc., in endless variety.

FISH.

Cool, pure, and abundant as is the water, there are but two varieties of fish in the Hills proper, the sucker and the dace.

In external appearance the sucker is the exact counterpart of the eastern fish, but it is entirely different in habits, in the fewness of its bones, and in the solidity and excellence of its flesh. It takes a grasshopper greedily, frequently rising to the top of the water like a trout. It makes a better fight, and furnishes much better sport than its eastern namesake, and is a most delicate and delicious addition to the bill of fare.

The dace rarely, if ever, exceeds half a pound in weight. Generally it is quite small, like mountain trout, which it also resembles in its habits and in its delicacy as food. It takes the fly admirably, and furnishes good sport.

In the Red Water and Spear-fish Creeks there is a very curious red sucker, with a snout greatly prolonged, which I have seen nowhere else.

The Spear-fish Creek especially abounds in suckers, the red and common varieties. It takes its name (a translation of the Indian name) from being a favorite fishing-place of the Indians, who frequently resort to it, and kill great numbers of fish by spearing them with lances and arrows.

In the Red Water, below its junction with Spear-fish, and also in the Belle Fourche, there are great numbers of the "lady," "channel," or "spotted" cat-fish, a delicious fish, the trout of its kind. It is very strong, bites vigorously, and makes an excellent fight. The largest one killed by any of our party weighed nearly six pounds, and, singular to relate, it was taken without a reel, on a very small trout-fly.

In these two streams there are also great numbers of a white fish, very long, very narrow, and very deep through. It is exceedingly voracious, taking any bait offered, and pulling with great force. It is very like a fish commonly called in North Carolina the "hickory shad."

REPTILES.

In the higher portions of the Black Hills there are no snakes. A few were seen in the valley of Rapid Creek, and on one or two of the other streams I saw a very small variety of water moccasin, scarcely a foot in length. Reptiles of any kind are very scarce; a few specimens of only the following were seen: rattlesnake, garter snake, water moccasin, marsh frog, striped-head turtle, and a curious fish-lizard common to the plains.

In the Red Valley and plains skirting the Hills, rattlesnakes were found in considerable numbers.

INSECTS

are exceedingly numerous, and in very great variety. That pest of the frontier settler, the grasshopper, breeds here in immense numbers. They do no perceptible damage, and leave the Hills as soon as they get their wings.

Horse-flies and other biting flies are very numerous and in many varieties, and were excessively annoying to our horses and mules.

The common house-fly is abundant, and the buzzing blue-bottle more numerous and persistent than I have elsewhere seen them.

The dead pine breeds a curious red-bellied bug, a little like a large ant, which penetrates everywhere, and bites sharply when interfered with.

HUNTING.

In spite of the comparative scarcity of game, already mentioned, I have never seen a more perfect hunting country, nor enjoyed hunting more thoroughly, than in the Black Hills last summer and fall. The game was in little variety, and not very abundant, but there was sufficient to give most admirable sport to the hunter; and having had no previous experience in taking care of itself, it was not difficult to bag by a skillful sportsman.

Of all the game animals, red deer were in greatest abundance and more widely diffused, and from the moment of our entering the Hills scarcely a day passed without our seeing some of these beautiful animals, many of which contributed to our already well-supplied larder.

The game, however, not being in season, and all of our party having work to do, there was very little hunting, except by men regularly detailed for that purpose from the companies, until after the middle of July.

About the 20th of that month, our party being at Camp Crook, on Rapid Creek, we were visited by General Crook and quite a party of citizen friends, all anxious to see the country, and eager for a hunt in its virgin forests.

We started at one o'clock one afternoon, went ten miles, and camped on the head waters of a small tributary of Box-Elder, the party bagging six red deer before dark. The next day all the guests were out, and by night all returned, bringing altogether one elk, one mountain sheep, and sixteen red deer.

Next morning all were out again before the sun, and though working necessarily over the same ground hunted on the day before, all were in by noon, bringing fifteen red deer. We returned the same afternoon to Camp Crook, having bagged in the two days' hunt one elk, one mountain sheep, and thirty-seven deer, which, considering that some of the hunters had never before seen a deer alive, was, in my opinion, a remarkable bag.

The hunting was entirely "still" hunting, there not being a dog in the party. The woods and thickets were very dense. Deer are remarkably tenacious of life, and in this hunt more deer got into the thickets and were lost to the hunters after being mortally wounded, than were bagged.

Had each hunter been accompanied by a well-broken dog, our bag would have been more than doubled.

The difference in size of the red deer of the Black Hills is very remarkable. A few days previous to the arrival of General Crook, I killed near Rapid Creek two enormous bucks, each of which, after disemboweling, and having head and legs cut off, weighed nearly one hundred and thirty pounds. In the hunt on Box-Elder, one of the guests killed a buck just as old and just as fat as those killed by me on Rapid, but which, dressed in the same way, weighed scarcely forty pounds.

It is exceedingly difficult to account for this variation in size. They are undoubtedly the same animal, as the large and small are found running together in herds or bands, in which are represented all the gradations in size between the extremes mentioned. In my opinion, it is simply a freak of nature, no more to be accounted for than the difference in size among men.

On the 13th August Camp Crook was abandoned, and we passed at once into that portion of the Black Hills most abounding in game.

Though too much occupied in hunting road for the

wagons to devote much time to game, yet scarcely a day passed in the next month that did not add from one to three deer to my bag.

Just at the north rim, the black-tailed deer were found in considerable numbers, and many were bagged. I one day bagged two splendid black-tail bucks with a single rifle ball. Another day I bagged two red deer at a single shot. Though I have tried hard many times before, these are the only two occasions of my life on which I bagged two deer with one bullet.

Elk, too, were quite plenty in the country about the northern rim. This animal, the easiest of all game beasts to bag in open ground, is the most difficult in thickets. His senses are more acute than those of any other animal, and however little hunted, the cracking of a twig or rustling of dry leaves will put him on the alert, and if continued, send him into densest cover.

He is very timid, and for so large and apparently unwieldly an animal, a most extraordinary adept at hiding.

Should he see, hear, or smell an enemy at a distance, he will silently steal away, so noiselessly that the hunter is not aware of his vicinity. But should the hunter come by accident very close to him, he will stand perfectly motionless in the thicket, relying for his safety on his skill in hiding.

One of our hunters followed a large elk trail into a little valley filled with a dense jungle. Cautiously pushing his way in for some distance, he suddenly became aware of the presence of an elk. The animal was facing him, only a few feet off, so near, indeed, that he might have touched it with his gun. His head, crowned with magnificent antlers, was close to the ground; and, watching out of the corners of his eyes, the buck stood perfectly motionless.

In the excitement of this rather dangerous-looking apparition the hunter fired, missing entirely or only slightly wounding the elk.

At the report of the gun, the whole valley was alive with rushing animals; at least a hundred, crashing through the brush, disappeared up the mountain side.

The hunter had got unwittingly into the very midst of the herd.

Only about a dozen elk were bagged by our whole party during the trip. I killed three, but bagged but one.

These thickets are also the abode of numbers of bears, from the little black to the mammoth grizzly. Only seven or eight bears were killed by our whole party, owing to our lack of dogs. The bear will not leave the cover of the thickets, and to attack a grizzly or even a brown bear in his lair, is sport entirely too exciting for the average hunter. I saw but one bear during the whole trip, and got a long shot at him, but he escaped into a dense pine thicket.

The country in this part of the Hills is full of bear "sign." In some places almost a quarter of an acre will be rooted up as if by hogs; small thickets of berry-bearing bushes are torn and broken; ant-hills are dug into and huge logs turned over by this omnivorous monster in search of his food.

It was absolutely dangerous to go into the dense jungles, where, unable to see, and almost to move, the hunter was entirely at the mercy of an animal so powerful and so ferocious when disturbed.

Two or three cougars, the mountain or California lion, were seen by members of our party, but none killed. This animal rarely leaves his lair by day, but prowls about the camps at night, his footsteps in the soft earth frequently proving a proximity too close to be pleasant in so powerful a beast, were he not known to be a most arrant coward.

The wolves are of enormous size, and in considerable numbers. This special variety is called the "timber" wolf. It is a very dark gray in color, heavily and strongly built, and is regarded by frontiermen as more dangerous than even the great gray wolf of the northern prairies.

All wolves are very cowardly, and will run from the smallest cur. In many years' experience on the frontier I have never known, or even heard, of any man being attacked or in any way injured by a wolf of any size or character.

On the plains to the east of the Hills antelope are very abundant, and many were bagged by the party.

While the expeditionary force was encamped at Warren's Spring, in the Red Valley, on the east side of the Hills, I made a last hunt of three days, on our old favorite hunting-ground, the Box-Elder.

On one of these days I made the best hunt of my life, killing eight deer out of ten seen.

I have killed more deer in a day, but never so large a proportion of those encountered.

As evidence of the nutritious character of the grasses on the east side of the Hills, I must mention the fact that our wagon-train aroused a black-tailed buck from his bed in a little brake on a hillside, which was so fat as to be unable to run, and scarcely to trot.

One of the train-guards on foot ran up to the animal, as it attempted to waddle off, and killed it, the muzzle of his rifle almost touching the deer.

All the animals on this side of the Hills were enormously fat, but none to so helpless an extent as this.

It was not to the rifle alone that we were indebted for sport. Our shot-guns were frequently called into requisition, adding not a little to our pleasures both in the field and at table.

Inside the Hills shot-gun shooting is scarcely exciting enough to be interesting, the "sport" necessarily being of the "pot-hunter" character.

The grouse were only found in dense thickets, and when disturbed, fluttered into the low branches of trees, from which they could be driven with difficulty. All could be shot, of course; indeed, they were so tame that some were killed with sticks and stones—but there was no wing shooting.

So also with the young mallard ducks. Many could be killed, but only in the water or grass.

Very different was the shooting in the Red Valley, in the outer rampart, along the Belle Fourche, and the streams of the east side.

Occasionally a pack of sage grouse was found, which gave splendid sport, this bird being strong on the wing. Our best sport was, however, from the sharp-tail grouse. This bird is similar in size and general appearance to the pinnated grouse (or prairie chicken of the Western States). It is, however, lighter in color; it lacks the neck-feathers, from which the pinnated grouse takes its name; its legs are more thickly covered with feathers, and the two center feathers of the tail are an inch or more longer and very much stiffer than the others. Great numbers were found along the north and east foot-hills, and furnished most excellent sport.

In the fall of the year all the water-courses are

covered with myriads of geese and ducks, and numbers were killed by our party.

Shot-gun shooting is only an aggravating sport without a dog, and even at best I confess my preference for the rifle.

A lieutenant with our command had two fine sporting dogs, and being an excellent shot and indefatigable hunter, bagged immense numbers of fine birds.

Taken altogether, the hunting in and near the Black Hills is better than the average.

INDIANS AND THE INDIAN QUESTION.

It is believed by some persons that the Crow Indians, the former owners, actually occupied and lived in the Black Hills before being driven out by the Sioux. I do not think so, for two reasons: First, If this country had been used as a residence, even thirty years ago, some marks of its occupation would still be visible. Second, The mountain Crows are known to be determined fighters, in their own fastnesses. Had even a small band occupied and defended the Hills, they could have held it until now against the whole Sioux nation, who, though excellent horseback fighters, are worth nothing on foot; and though most dangerous, aggressive enemies on the plains, are timid as hares in woods and mountains.

My opinion is, that the Black Hills have never been a permanent home for any Indians. Even now small parties go a little way into the Hills to cut spruce lodge-poles, but all the signs indicate that these are mere sojourns of the most temporary character.

The "teepe," or lodge, may be regarded as the Indian's house, the wickyup as his tent. One is his permanent residence, the other the make-shift shelter for a night. Except in one single spot, near the head of Castle Creek, I saw nowhere any evidence whatever of a lodge having been set up, while old wickyups were not unfrequent in the edge of the Hills. There is not one single teepe or lodge-pole trail, from side to side of the Hills, in any direction, and these poles, when dragged in the usual way by ponies, soon make a trail as difficult to obliterate as a wagon road, visible for many years, even though not used.

Several small parties of Indians, overcome by curiosity, and reassured by the presence of the "soldiers," came into the Hills this summer. The most intelligent of these, an Indian named Robe Raiser, was quite communicative, and informed the interpreter that, though fifty years old, and though he had been around the Hills almost every year of his life, he had never before ventured inside; that when passing north or south in the fall, the squaws come in sometimes to cut lodge-poles, the bucks venturing to hunt a little, but that these stops are very short. His reasons for the Indians not coming in were: First, That the Hills are "bad medicine," and the abode of spirits. Second, That there is nothing to come for except lodge-poles, the game being scarce and more difficult to kill than that on the plains. Third, That the thickets are so dense that their ponies are soon lost if turned loose, and the flies are so bad that they are tormented and worried out, if kept tied up. Fourth, That it rains very frequently, and that the Indian does not like rain. Fifth, That it thunders and lightens with terrible force, tearing trees to pieces and setting fire to the woods. He said, moreover, that the Indians had never lived here, and did not and would not live here now; that they did not want the country, and would have sold or given it away long ago to the whites, but for the "squaw men" about the reservations, who urged them to make a "big fuss" and they would be sure to get a "big price" for the country.

These statements are borne out by those of every Indian communicated with, and by the observation of every man of our party. The Indians do not live in, occupy, or use the country in any way (except for lodge-poles, as stated); they do not want it; the large majority would willingly give it to the whites, but for the exertions and influence of as rascally a set of white men as curse the earth. It appears probable that there will be a war on this question. Some homes will be ruined, some good men and valuable citizens will be murdered, some women ravished, some babies brained against burning door-posts, and all because a few miscreants want to make money.

The Black Hills are closed to settlers by virtue of a treaty with the Indians, which treaty, the settlers claim, has been violated by the Indians time and again. By it the Indians agreed to abstain from robbery and murder of the whites. Within a very short time after it was made, the very Indians making it murdered an officer of the army, and though (I am told) the individual Indians who committed the crime are well known, though the jewelry and other articles of the murdered man are worn openly by the murderers, not only is nothing said about it, but the murderers and their families are "good Indians," living at the reservation and drawing their rations with excellent regularity.

Every year since the treaty was signed has witnessed more or less pillage, depredation, and murder, by the treaty Indians. This year several hundred head of valuable brood mares were run off from the Laramie plains. The Indians from the Agencies made no less than four pillaging expeditions to the Loup this summer, and about the 1st of October, a young man, peaceably herding cattle on Cottonwood Creek, not far from the post of Fort Laramie, was set upon, killed, and scalped by a party of friendly Indians from the Agencies. These facts, and many similar ones, are perfectly known to the men who wish to settle the Black Hills, and, whether justly or not, they inveigh with great bitterness against a treaty which prevents them from going into and taking possession of Indian territory, but does not prevent the Indian from coming to their farms in the settlements, murdering them, or carrying off their property.

It may appear very singular to most persons that a question so easy of solution as this Indian problem should have been allowed to disturb and agitate the country for so many years.

It must appear strange, the facts being known to almost every intelligent person of the land, that agents of the Government have been permitted to starve and swindle the Indian year after year with impunity.

The murder of a family by white ruffians, with the accompaniment of rape and arson, would send a thrill of horror through every breast. No stone would be left unturned to capture the villains and bring them to the gallows. Yet every year murders, arsons, rapes are permitted to the Indian as pastimes, the murderers, though known, not only remaining unmolested, but being fed and petted by the agents of a Government which owes protection to all its citizens.

The impunity which surrounds all these abuses is, however, easily accounted for, when we reflect on the enormous power of money, and the desperate passion with which some men pursue gain.

There is more money in this Indian question than in any other which agitates the country, and where money is, there power is also.

Some of the greatest fortunes of this country have been founded on Indian contracts, Indian agencies, Indian trade.

Some of our wealthiest and most powerful citizens are, at this moment, pecuniarily interested in having this matter remain just as it is, and the Indian Ring is the wealthiest and most powerful in the land.

I shall say no more on this most important and interesting subject, having fully discussed the question, from my stand-point, in a book "The Plains," which will soon be in press.

ROUTES TO BLACK HILLS.

In their efforts to avoid the troops, the miners last summer went into the Black Hills by every possible and seemingly impossible route. Some went up the Niobrara; others up the White; others again up the Cheyenne. A few parties crossed the Platte far up toward Fort Fetterman, coming into the Hills from the west; while one most venturesome party took steamboat up the Missouri river, landed in the wilderness above the mouth of the Cheyenne river, and made its devious and tedious way across the bad lands north of that stream.

There are, consequently, many routes to the Black Hills which may or will be used by parties seeking to evade arrest.

I have no advice or instruction for that class of persons.

My recommendation as to route supposes that the Black Hills will be opened to settlers and miners, and that no hiding or evasion is necessary.

The question of route is a simple one, depending on where the traveler starts from, and what his outfit.

Should the party start from Minnesota or northern Iowa with teams or pack-mules, the best point from which to make the plunge into the wilderness is Sioux City. A wagon road leads up the Niobrara and into the Hills from the southeast.

This is a long and tedious journey, trying to men and animals, and dangerous from Indians.

I would recommend no one to take it except those who cannot spare the time to take the only really practicable route, up the Platte river.

For all persons east and south of the mouth of the Platte, there is really but the one route. Those east, crossing at Omaha, follow up the Platte; those south, striking the Platte at Kearney or elsewhere, continue up that stream.

The old Mormon road furnishes a good route, preferable in every way to the Niobrara route, except that it is somewhat longer. The road is better for the whole distance, and being comparatively within reach of civilization, there is very little danger from Indians.

As far as the junction of the two Plattes, the traveler constantly passes settlements and railroad stations. Assistance can be had in case of sickness, broken wagons can be repaired, and lost animals replaced.

From North Platte station, two routes are open to the traveler. He can follow the old Mormon road up the North Platte. This is the nearest road, but has not been much used for some years, and is likely out of repair. It also takes the traveler away from the settlements sooner than there is necessity. The best route is up Pole Creek, along the railroad to Sidney.

From Sidney two routes, both fairly good, lead to the Black Hills; the one, *via* the Agencies, the other, *via* Cheyenne.

The route *via* the Agencies is a very fair wagon road. It runs a little west of north, crossing the North Platte near Court-House Rock, to Camp Robinson (Red Cloud Agency), one hundred and nineteen miles; then slightly east of north, down Hat Creek to the Cheyenne river, thence west of north again. Total distance from Sidney to Custer City, about two hundred and five miles.

This is very considerably the nearest route for parties having their own wagons or pack-mule trains, but it is not nearly so good as the longer one, *via* Cheyenne.

There is no bridge on the North Platte, and the crossing is a bad one; there is a good deal of heavy sand between the North Platte and the Niobrara; the route from Camp Robinson to the Cheyenne is through "bad lands," almost impassable in wet weather; water is scarce along the route, and in some places very alkaline and bad; grass is generally poor, and wood almost entirely lacking.

The other route continues along the regularly traveled road, near the railroad, to Cheyenne City.

From Cheyenne City, the road runs slightly east of north ninety miles to Fort Laramie, thence in the same general direction by Rawhide Peak and Cheyenne river to Custer City, one hundred and thirty-five miles. Total distance from Cheyenne City, two hundred and twenty-five miles. Parties from the East with their own wagons or pack-mules will find this very considerably the longer, but in every other respect very greatly the better route.

They will arrive at stations or settlements at convenient distances apart for camping, all the way to

This Page is Blank

Materials were not available when scanned.

Fort Laramie, or to within one hundred and thirty-five miles of their destination.

The road is well traveled and most excellent. There are good bridges over both the Laramie and North Platte rivers. The water along the route beyond Fort Laramie is at very convenient intervals for camping, and invariably good, except at Beaver Creek. The grass is everywhere very fine, and wood sufficient everywhere except on the Niobrara.

Except in distance, the route *via* Cheyenne is decidedly best in every way.

Three or four miles beyond the Niobrara this road forks. The right hand goes direct to Custer City and the heart of the eastern section of the Hills. The left hand, *via* Camp Jenney, to the northwestern section and all the newly discovered "diggings."

To parties who go out by railroad, expecting to outfit themselves at the last station, I recommend Cheyenne City as the starting-point. That is a much larger town than Sidney. There are more stores, more competition, and their purchases will be made to better advantage. Animals, wagons, tools, etc., are quite as cheap and more plentiful than at Sidney.

The moment the Hills are opened several lines of stages will be put on the route from Cheyenne City to Custer City, all preparations having already been made. I have been informed by the proprietor of one of these contemplated lines, that he intends his stages to make the distance from Fort Laramie to Custer City in twenty-four hours.

RETURN ROUTE.

On October 3d we crossed the Cheyenne river for the last time, and, with many regrets, turned our backs on the Black Hills. Our route led directly across a section of the tertiary deposits common to this country, and known to plains-men as the "Bad Lands." These deposits vary in thickness in different localities, from thirty to five hundred feet, and appear to be based on a generally level plain. The great peculiarity of the soil is, that the rains cut myriads of ravines, with nearly perpendicular sides, partially or completely through the whole depth of the deposit. In course of time, the tops of the walls between contiguous ravines are eaten away by water and frost, leaving sharp ridges or back-bones —"hogs' backs." These are gradually washed away, until more or less of the bottom is a comparative level.

In the first two stages, "Bad Lands" are impassable. In the last stage, good routes may be found in dry weather; in wet, it becomes boggy and almost impassable. From the Cheyenne river we mounted a high bluff to a level mésa. Crossing this for a couple of miles, we came suddenly upon the edge of an immense bowl-shaped depression in the earth, eight to ten miles in diameter, and the sides from one hundred and fifty to five hundred feet deep. These sides are cut by water into every conceivable form. Where we struck the edge there was no possibility of getting our trains down, while the bottom presented only "hogs' backs" in their most aggravated form. Skirting the edge, we finally found a place where we could get down. Most fortunately for us the "Bad Lands" were here in the last and best stage, and we succeeded in getting through with little trouble.

No one can imagine or realize, from any picture or description, the wonderful and weird beauty of a view in the Bad Lands.

Almost the whole country between the Cheyenne and White rivers is filled with these irregular depressions, separated from each other by walls of greater or less thickness, while dotted over the bottom of each are thousands of isolated castles, towers, domes, obelisks, pyramids, carved by water and frescoed in various colored earths. These are the "bone fields," the burying-ground of races extinct before the advent of man. Bones of every size and shape represent an infinite variety of forms, from the diminutive three-toed horse of twenty inches to the mastodon of twenty feet in height.

Within these "Bad Lands" there is nothing for

the settler; no timber, no stone, no grass, no water, no soil.

Following up the White river for some miles we finally escape the dreary and desolate wonders of the "Bad Lands," and enter upon a country excellent for stock-raising.

The White river (five hundred miners' inches) is here a stream of whitish water, pure and good, flowing in a shallow bed of one hundred feet in width. The mésa encroaches greatly, leaving but a narrow "bottom," which, however, is of rich soil, and quite thickly covered with cotton-wood, some of the trees being very old and large. Bottom and upland are all covered with a thick coat of excellent grass. The country has not arable land enough to make it of any special value agriculturally, but it will support large herds of cattle. Going up twenty miles further, the river changes its character from a shallow stream, running swiftly over a broad bed, to a narrow, sluggish, rather nasty-looking canal, several feet in depth, with steep banks and miry bottom. For a hundred miles, to the Red Cloud Agency, this stream preserves these general characteristics. It is a splendid grazing country, though the grass was somewhat eaten off by the great numbers of Indian ponies which had been along it, going to or returning from the Council. There is a considerable quantity of good pine timber on the hills back from the stream, and this country will be a good one for settlers as soon as the Indian can be got rid of.

The troops at the posts near the Indian Reservations on White river or tributaries have excellent gardens, and raise fine corn and vegetables without irrigation.

The Niobrara, a fine stream of eight hundred miners' inches, and increasing in volume with great rapidity, has a wide "bottom" of excellent soil, thickly covered with splendid grass. It will support vast herds of cattle, but there is not a particle of timber on the river, nor building-stone near it, for many miles of its course.

The northwestern portion of Nebraska is a valuable country in many respects, and will furnish comfortable homes for a population as dense as almost any other portion of the High Plains.

On the 13th October we arrived at Fort Laramie. Our delightful pic-nic was ended, and the pleasant companionship of several months broken up.

CONCLUSION.

The "Black Hills" country is a true oasis in a wide and dreary desert. The approaches from every direction are through long stretches of inhospitable plains, treeless and broken, in which the supply of water is so saturated with bitter and nauseous alkalies as to be unfit for the continuous use of the white man.

Nature seems to have been at pains to set barriers around and about it. The barren plains, cut with innumerable ravines and gorges, the nauseous water, are succeeded on a nearer approach by sharp, steep, almost impassable ridges and cañons, in which scarce any water is to be found.

Every step towards the heart of these "sacred fastnesses" is beset with innumerable difficulties. These overcome, the venturous explorer is amply repaid for all his hardships and privations. Almost any moderately good country would seem a "Paradise" after passing the "Purgatory" of such approaches to it; but, allowing for the full extravagance of pleasure which the traveler must feel under such circumstances, after mature judgment derived from several months of actual sojourn, and the cool comparison which a return to civilization enables me to make, I but express my fair and candid opinion when I pronounce the Black Hills, in many respects, the finest country I have ever seen.

The beauty and variety of the scenery, the excellence of the soil, the magnificence of the climate, the abundance of timber and building-stone, make it a most desirable residence for men who want good homes.

As a grazing country it cannot be surpassed; and small stock-farms of fine cattle and sheep cannot, I think, fail of success.

In a few years, when this wilderness shall have been made to "blossom as the rose," with cozy farms and comfortable residences, when rocky crags shall have been crowned with palatial hotels, the tourist will find an ample reward in climbing the rugged heights, or exploring the dark defiles of this wonderful land.

Gold there is, everywhere in the granitic areas; gold enough to make many fortunes, and tempt to the loss of many more. The very uncertainty has a fascination for many men. It is a grand lottery! Only a few draw prizes, but each may be the favorite of the "fickle goddess."

This hope, this barest chance, will draw thousands of men from comfortable homes and sorrowing friends.

In a few weeks or months the eager thirst for "pot-holes" will have deserted the better class, and they will settle down into valuable citizens of a country destined in a few years to be an important and wealthy portion of the great American Republic.

THE END.

Woıks of Elizabeth Barrett Browning.

Diamond Edition. Complete in 1 vol., 16mo, cloth, $1.50. Half calf, extra, $3.00. Full calf, or morocco, ... **$3.75**

Red Line Edition. Complete in 1 vol. With twelve original full-page illustrations, by SOL. EYTINGE, Jr., W. J. HENNESSY, C. G. BUSH, and W. THWAITES. Small quarto, elegantly bound ın cloth, gilt, $4.50. Half calf, extra, $6.00. Full calf, or morocco, ... **8.00**

Crown 8vo Edition. An entirely new edition, with portrait. Large type, complete. 2 vols., 8vo, cloth, ... **5.00**

Globe Edition, 12mo, printed on fine tinted paper, handsomely bound in beveled boards. 3 vols. **7.50**

Library, or **Aldine Edition,** 12mo, bound in brown cloth, printed on tinted paper. 4 vols. . **9.00**

Cabinet Edition, 16mo, printed on tinted paper, bound in green cloth. 5 vols. **8.75**

Blue and Gold Edition. 32mo. 5 vols. . . . **6.25**

Green and Gold Edition. 32mo. 5 vols. . **6.25**

Aurora Leigh. 32mo. Blue and gold. . . **1.25**

Do. 16mo. Green cloth. **1.75**

Last Poems. 32mo. Blue and Gold **1.25**

Do. 16mo. Green cloth. **1.75**

Any of the above can be had in a variety of Fine Bindings.

☞ Sent free on receipt of price. ☜

VALUABLE BOOKS FOR FAMILIES AND SCHOOLS.

Science of Familiar Things. A GUIDE TO THE SCIENTIFIC KNOWLEDGE OF THINGS FAMILIAR. By the Rev. Dr. BREWER, Head Master of King's College School, Norwich. Carefully revised and adapted for use in Families and Schools in the United States. One thick volume. Price.. $1 25

This Volume contains about 2,000 Questions and Answers, explaining, in the most concise and intelligible manner, the phenomena of every-day occurrence. It contains an amount of useful information never before collected in a shape so convenient for study, and so easy for reference.

EXTRACT FROM PREFACE.—"No science is generally more interesting than that which explains the common phenomena of life. We see that salt and snow are both white, a rose red, leaves green, and the violet a deep purple; but how few persons ever ask the reason why! We know that a flute produces a musical sound, and a cracked bell a discordant one—that fire is hot, ice cold, and a candle luminous—that water boils when subjected to heat, and freezes from cold; but when a child looks up into our face and asks us 'why,'—how many times is it silenced with a frown, or called 'very foolish for asking such silly questions!' The object of the present book is to explain about two thousand of these questions, (which are often more easily asked than answered,) in language so simple that a child may understand it, yet not so childish as to offend the scientific. In order to secure the strictest accuracy in the answers, the most approved modern authors have been consulted, and each edition has been submitted to the revision of gentlemen of acknowledged reputation for scientific attainments. The almost unparalleled success of this little volume, of which 120,000 copies have been printed since the year 1848, is an incontrovertible proof of its acceptability; and has induced the author to spare neither labor nor expense to render his 'Guide to the Scientific Knowledge of Things Familiar' instructive and amusing to the young, as well as to those of maturer life.

A Course of English Reading. Adapted to Various Tastes and Capacities. *Based on the Manual of Rev. J. Pycroft, of Trinity College, Oxford.* By J. A. SPENCER, S. T. D., of the College of the City of New York. 12mo, cloth. Price.. $1 25

"NEVER TOO LATE TO LEARN."

Five Hundred Mistakes of Daily Occurrence, in Speaking, Pronouncing, and Writing the English Language, Corrected.

"Which—if you but open—
You will be unwilling,
For many a shilling,
To part with the profit
Which you shall have of it."
(*The Key to Unknown Knowledge.—London*, 1569.)

12mo, cloth extra. Price.. 80 cts.

NEW WORK ON SYNONYMS.

Hand-Book of English Synonyms, and Proverbs and Phrases from the Latin, French, Spanish, and Italian Languages. With Tables of Weights and Measures, and the Value of Money of all Commercial Nations. 16mo, cloth. Price.. $1 00

Macaulay's Lays of Ancient Rome. A Classic Reader. School Edition. 16mo, cloth. Price.. $1 25

Drawing Book for Young Children. Containing One Hundred and Fifty Drawing Copies, and numerous *exercises*, with directions. (Published under the Superintendence of the Society for the Diffusion of Useful Knowledge, London.) Small quarto, cloth. Price..................$1 25

Plato's Phædo; *or, The Immortality of the Soul.* Translated from the Greek, by CHARLES S. STANFORD. With a Life of Plato, by ARCHBISHOP FENÉLON. 12mo, cloth. Price............ ....$1 25

Paley's Evidences of Christianity. With Annotations by RICHARD WHATELEY, D. D., Archbishop of Dublin. Octavo, cloth. Price....... ....$2 50

Rochefoucauld's Maxims and Moral Reflections; also, Shakspearean Aphorisms. 16mo, cloth. Price.......................... ... $1 25

"MANNERS MAKE THE MAN."

HAND-BOOKS OF ETIQUETTE.

The Gentleman's Manual of Etiquette, and Guide to Polite Society.
16mo, cloth. Price..... .... 75 cts

The Lady's Hand-Book of Etiquette, and Manual of Politeness.
16mo, cloth. Price.............. ....75 cts.

The Complete Hand-Book of Etiquette for Ladies and Gentlemen.
16mo, cloth. Price.............. .... 75 cts.

HOW TO WRITE CORRECTLY.

The Fashionable Letter-Writer. Original and Selected, containing a variety of Letters on Love, Courtship, Marriage, Relationship, Business, Friendship, etc.; with Forms of Complimentary Cards. Also, Directions for Letter-Writing. 16mo, boards. Price.......... ...... 60 cts.

The Gentleman's Letter-Writer. Embodying Letters of Love and Courtship; of Friendship; about Education; of Business; of Invitation, etc. Also, a copious Appendix of Forms, Bills, Receipts, and other useful matter. 18mo, cloth. Price... ....60 cts.

The Lady's Letter-Writer. Embracing Letters on Love and Matrimony; to Relatives and Friends; to obtain Situations; Notes of Invitation, etc., with an Appendix of Forms, Bills, Receipts, and other useful matter. 18mo, cloth. Price.. ....60 cts.

The Parlor Letter-Writer. Original and Selected, to which is also added a List of Syncnyms of the English Language. 16mo, cloth. Price $1 00

www.ingramcontent.com/pod-product-compliance
Lightning Source LLC
LaVergne TN
LVHW011229110826
845150LV00006B/1581